HOW DO I

HOW DO I PRAY?

Edited by
Robert Heyer

All rights reserved. No part of this book may be reproduced or transmitted in any form or by any means, electronic or mechanical, including photocopying, recording or by any information storage and retrieval system, without permission in writing from the Publisher.

PAULIST PRESS

New York / Ramsey / Toronto

The articles in this book originally appeared in *New Catholic World.*
Copyright © 1977 by The Missionary Society of St. Paul the Apostle in
the State of New York.

Art and Design: Gloria Ortíz

Library of Congress
Catalog Card Number: 77-80808

ISBN: 0-8091-2041-0

Published by Paulist Press
Editorial Office: 1865 Broadway, N.Y., N.Y. 10023
Business Office: 545 Island Road, Ramsey, N.J. 07446

Printed and bound in the United States of America

CONTENTS

TWENTY-EIGHT OUTSTANDING
CHRISTIANS ANSWER THE QUESTION:

HOW DO I PRAY?

"A child shall lead them."

DORIS DONNELLY

The birth of any child is a radical interruption in the way we live, in the style of life we've become accustomed to. Part of the irony and part of the mystery of the birth of Jesus is that a *child* can command so much attention, can demand so much commitment, can so alter priorities and can so turn lives up-

Doris Donnelly holds a Ph.D. in theology from the Claremont Graduate School and presently teaches at Princeton Theological Seminary.

side down and inside out. Any parent can confirm the prophet's words that "a child shall lead them" (Is. 11:6). Children just do.

The arrival of my own two children was an awesome event of such magnitude in my life that my prayer was radically and irreversibly affected as a result. From the very beginning, Christopher and Peggy instructed me in prayer—

helping me to simplify it, to wonder at it, to hunger for it. Their instruction was rigorous and lovely, like prayer itself, and I found life with my Lord energized by a new power that was mediated by the mystery and presence of my son and daughter.

Time

I think that at the base of the motherhood experience was a new dealing with *time*: simple time that I never had enough of before my first child Christopher was born, but at least was able to command, now seemed out of my control. And there just wasn't enough of it. The little time there was was never "mine": no time to study, to read, to do anything leisurely. I was astounded at how jealously I had guarded, squandered and controlled time before and how selfish I had been about doling out segments of it to others.

In the process of my preoccupation with time, I learned something new about it: that time was a gift—probably the singlemost important gift that I could offer my family and friends. *My* time. Agenda-less time. Just being with those I loved; taking time.

I began to reorder my life. I "found" time, "made" time for those who were important to me and then just enjoyed minutes, hours, and days with those I loved. It was an extravagance I never knew before. There *was* time, and I was doing with it exactly what I wanted—gifting it to those who mattered very much to me just so I could be with them.

I was reimpressed with the factual truth about the time that Jesus gave: that he came in time. The paradox is precisely that the absolute gratuity of revelation is characterized by historical contingency. Time. He gave a life in *our* time and will give us a life in *his* time. I was glad to be part of that history and that future.

I've come to understand prayer as taking time to be with someone closer to me than I am to myself. To be with another, *the* Other, with no plan, no project, nothing particular to be accomplished. Simply *to be* so that listening to the other's movements and mine is possible. Sometimes these are speechless times when just being in the presence of God is adequate. In these moments I am helped by remembering how I have known the wordless presence of my children in the same room with me to be so stirring and so immediate that to distract that event with words would be to dilute the loveliness of the experience. The great moments come when the movements are synchronous—when there is an understanding that lets two hearts beat almost as one.

Christopher and Peggy have taught me that loving takes time. Loving God takes time. Human love takes time. Unhurried and exquisite and fitting in between appointments and errands, there is nothing I cherish more than time for prayer and for all other intimacies with those I love.

Wonder

A second surprise in store for me as a parent was the fascination of it all. In the early days, I frequently stood outside myself watching myself gasp at each of my children's accomplishments, at each change, wondering whether all parents saw these things in their children and puzzling why no one had told me how stunning it would all be. It would have been hard to believe; in fact, I would have doubted that I could have been so affected.

Because of the children, I found myself more and more attentive to detail and more capable of being surprised. My focus was each child who remained unyielding in demanding my total, undivided attention but who compensated for this tyranny by being so utterly "new." Once Christopher and Peggy were old enough to walk, each outing became an exercise in pondering the intricacies of the universe. Every crack in the sidewalk was examined for blades of grass and ants which were fondled by thumby hands that touched the world and its guests with chaste reverence. The trip from the front door of the house to the car was an adventure in unmasking the glory of God in its minute splendor.

The children's pace became my own. I unraveled the Word of God with a new gentleness and an exhilaration at the detail that was, that *is*, there. The massive, foolish, extravagant, compelling love of Jesus took on a new vibrancy and a new history. I claimed it with a familiarity and ease I had not known before. When the pace slowed down, there was more time to wonder and there was more time to contemplate. My life followed the pattern.

Relationships are kept alive by a capacity in us that lets us wonder. Wonder enables us beyond curiosity to see people as God does and to love them in their uniqueness with a love we never thought ourselves capable of. Wonder is a necessary ingredient in the composition of prayer. It enables us to let the great mysteries of Christ's life dwell within us. The flow of prayer seems to demand that God direct us, form us, mold and inspire us, and this is what we allow to happen when we take our eyes from ourselves and turn them to him. He, then, becomes the center of our loving attention, and in the process of his becoming the center of our lives, it becomes possible for us to become what we love.

My children taught me frequently and deeply about prayer. Their demands on my time helped me unclutter my life and to find time used more meaningfully. Their capacity for wonder unleashed new possibilities for that dormant ability in me. Their presence and persistence cleared the paths for their mother to be "born again." ●

"Rejoice in the Lord always... The Lord is near."

JOSEPH C. McKINNEY

St. Paul points out the fruits of prayer in the lives of the sons of God: "Rejoice in the Lord always. . . . The Lord is near. Dismiss all anxiety from your minds. Present your needs to God in every form of prayer and petitions full of gratitude. Then God's own peace . . . will stand guard over your hearts and minds, in Christ Jesus" (Philippians 4:4-7).

Today, prayer is exciting. It often used to be frustrating. It is exciting because it brings us into a whole new way of life. Jesus becomes our Lord; we sense

God's wonder and glory, and discover the freedom of the sons of God. It used to be frustrating because I felt inadequate at prayer. I had guilt feelings because I did not pray enough, or I did not pray "better." There was some practical heresy, a semi-Pelagian kind, when I acted as though prayer depended upon me. Prayer is really God's work in us. To pray we need the help of the Holy Spirit, and Jesus is pleased with our efforts to cooperate in faith.

In this article I want to reflect on some insights about prayer and God's place in our prayer. To me the most accurate description of prayer is that it is the "breath of the spirit." I once thought that prayer was primarily conversation with God and discovered that, whenever I was not producing words, I thought I was not praying. The word "breath" implies that there is something coming in . . . and something going out. A vibrant prayer life should achieve a balance of the two.

When we pray we are supposed to lift our mind and heart to God. The emphasis must be on God, and not just on lifting the mind and heart. Prayer can easily become self-centered if our focus is not on Jesus Christ the Lord. Jesus told us that we cannot serve both God and man. Our hearts can be compared to a throne room. There is only one throne in each heart, and the critical question is, "Who is on the throne? Is it I? Or is it Jesus Christ?" This is the critical question that we need to answer daily. When we enter prayer with Jesus on the throne, our prayer becomes much more beautiful and enriching. Most of us have discovered

Most Reverend Joseph C. McKinney, D.D. is Auxiliary Bishop of Grand Rapids.

that when the ego reigns in our heart, it only leads to frustration, desperation, unhappiness and self-pity. Somehow or other, we are never able to be masters of our own universe. Like Jesus, we must be servants, not proud Pharisees. When Jesus is truly Lord of our hearts because he is on the throne, we permit God to be God and we act as his creatures and adopted sons. Prayer expresses our dependence on God, our trust in him and our readiness to submit to the divine plan. When Jesus is not on the throne, we must begin with the prayer of repentance, as we do at Mass.

Prayer becomes rewarding when we learn how to listen. "Any man who desires to come to me will hear my words and put them into practice" (Lk. 6:47). Listening is the inhaling action of our soul. This became clear to me when I had to face a critical problem. I was dealing with an alcoholic who needed my help. I had spent a long time talking with him and found that it was not fruitful. That night I spent some time asking the Lord Jesus what he thought of the situation, and then just sat in stillness. Out of that stillness came a hunch—a hunch that I was to try again, but this time to try to bring my friend around to talking about the Lord Jesus Christ. I also had the hunch that I was to take authority and insist with an iron-fist-and-velvet-glove approach that it was time that he did something about his alcoholism. Today I call those hunches inspirations. Jesus was teaching me a lesson. In Alcoholics Anonymous circles they call it "tough love."

There was also a far more important lesson. Instead of telling God the way I thought things should go, I learned to let Jesus be the master of the situation. I had the sense that the Lord wanted to deal with this situation, and I was merely an instrument in submission to him. He had a mission to that person and he was calling me to be part of that mission. God blessed that action. Someone who had been an alcoholic for years had a change of heart. He is now functioning in a resurrection way.

Out of that instance came a new desire to listen. Listening to God means being anxious to discover his plan, to let him be Lord, to let him have an opportunity to talk to me and show me the way. That kind of prayer, I believe, is the secret to happiness. I used to think that I was not praying when I did not have words to address to God. Somehow or other, praying meant "manufacturing" words, finding beautiful ways of saying things to God because he wanted to hear from me. Now I know that the important thing in prayer is to come in union with him, when he can speak to me and I can speak to him. Prayer needs a rhythm, like inhaling and exhaling.

Listening is most important whenever we make a decision. This became dramatically clear when the parish where I am pastor faced a critical decision. We were searching for a new principal for our school. We had gone through a long selection process and had come up with three candidates. We found ourselves having real difficulty making a final decision. A moment came in that meeting when I realized that all the facts were out in the open. People were repeating themselves and not moving toward a decision. I made a suggestion that each of us spend three minutes in silence—two minutes to ask God to enlighten us, and one minute to decide what we would do individually if it were our sole responsibility. Each person sought divine guidance, and afterward we had a round-robin in which each person was asked to name

one person, without giving any reasons. To our surprise, all seven people came up with the same name. We all left that meeting convinced that we had chosen the man God had raised up to be the principal of our school. Even if other people did not understand and would criticize our decision, we knew that we were within the will of God and that he would bless it. That happened several years ago and I have had a chance to see the fruits of that decision. I know that it was of God.

This taught me another thing about prayer. It is hard to discover any decision in our life that we should not bring before the Lord. The mistake that I was constantly making was to presume that God would be with my decisions as long as I had apostolic intentions. Now I realize that every decision in life is an important occasion for prayer. "If any of you is without wisdom, let him ask it from the God who gives generously . . . and it will be given him. Yet he must ask in faith, never doubting" (Jas. 1:5-6).

The word "submission" is a key word to a listening Christian, because we are all under the mission that God has for our lives. Every decision should be brought before him. I now find that I have developed a prayerful way to approach all decisions. I believe that God expects me to gather information and do my best to make a wise decision. When I make a choice, it is always very important that I bring it in prayer before God and seek his will before it is finalized. When I come before him I sometimes see things in a totally different light, especially when there is a selfish motive. Sometimes there is a strong prompting that I should delay the decision or look for other factors; at other times there seems to be no difficulty. Once I have submitted a decision to God I can proceed, even if others do not understand. Once I know that I made the effort to be in submission to God, I believe that God will bless such a decision in his own special way. The fruits of this procedure bear out the contention.

Today I recognize that obedience is a power virtue. This is the great lesson from the prayer of Jesus in the garden of Gethsemane. His prayerful obedience triggered the great act of redemption, and today we know that living the Paschal Mystery is the key to the spiritual life. "Seek out instead his Kingship and the rest will follow in time" (Lk. 12:37).

Some years ago I learned the Jesus prayer. It is a beautiful form of prayer that has an ancient tradition in the Church. It is especially preserved and fostered in the Eastern Church. This rhythmic prayer requires a person to breathe the name of Jesus with every breath. An ejaculation is usually added. In the Eastern rite that ejaculation is: "Jesus, Son of God, have mercy on me, a sinner." I do not always use that particular phrase, but I do believe that the name of Jesus should be repeated with each breath, and his name should well up from the heart. As this form of prayer developed, I discovered that Jesus becomes present in a significant and powerful way. I am reminded of Peter in the Acts of the Apostles when he proclaimed to the people that he did not heal the lame beggar, but that it was in Jesus' name that it was accomplished. There is a special power in Jesus' name. It is not surprising that the early Church relied so consistently on acting and praying in Jesus' name. There evidently is a natural quality to the Jesus prayer that is utilized in Oriental cults. I suspect that false gods can also become present to the person

who repeats his mantra. That is only my theory, but I do firmly believe that when we pray the Jesus prayer, we can come into his presence and experience Jesus present in us. This is a very valuable prayer, especially in moments of desolation, when we do not know what to say, or when we feel guilty about not praying well enough. I like to use the Jesus prayer when I am alone in my car. It helps me "tune into" him and give him the opportunity to reveal himself in a more total and intimate way.

There is another form of prayer that arises from an interpretation of Matthew 18:19-20: "Again I tell you, if two of you join your voices on earth to pray for anything whatever, it shall be granted you by my Father in heaven. Where two or three are gathered in my name, there am I in their midst." Several years ago I was taught that this is a powerful way to make a petition. People who come together to pray should agree on the specific intention they want to place before the Lord. Sometimes it takes a while for a group of people to come to an agreement about a petition. When they do, it is important that all of them voice their prayer. They should explicitly mention the name of Jesus on their lips, and they should emphasize praise and thanksgiving, because God listens whenever two or more are gathered together in Jesus' name. Many are the times that I have experienced quick answers to this type of prayer. I believe the petition should be very explicit. I believe we must offer that prayer in total submission to his will. We must come before him as children of God and, like children, present our needs in simple trust. God usually answers these prayers and often in a dramatic way. I have seen people come together to pray with a man out of work for help in finding a job. He found work within a week. When people want help in making a decision, or are facing difficulties with sickness or relationships, I get a few people together and follow this form of prayer. We do not pray as individuals but pray as brothers and sisters, lifting our hearts and our voices, explicitly mentioning our prayer before one another in the name of Jesus with thanksgiving. This prayer is answered and it makes one truly aware that we can come before God, and that he does listen to us. Now when someone asks me to pray for an intention, I suggest that we pray together. It is our baptism, not ordination, that gives us the power to come before God as children. People need to be encouraged to overcome their inhibitions about praying together and to put their baptismal power to work.

One of my best lessons in prayer came from a mother. In the morning homily we reflected upon the Lord's advice that we become like little children. That day her daughter was playing in the living room when she noticed her father sitting in his easy chair reading the paper. She interrupted her play, went to the closet and brought out a broken toy. She then approached her father, got his attention by tapping on his knee, and handed him the toy. With trusting eyes she looked at him and said, "Fix it?" A simple nod from him was enough. The mother noted that her daughter did not tell him how to fix it or set a time when she expected him to do it; she trusted him and handed the toy to him. Today I often use the "fix it" prayer. A few words in childlike trust are more important than our finest rhetoric when it comes to prayer. "Your heavenly Father knows all you need. Seek first his Kingdom over you, his way of holiness, and all these things will be given to you be-

sides. Enough then of worrying about tomorrow'' (Mt. 6:32-34).

Praying in tongues has become one of the most rewarding forms of prayer in my life. It is a gift of the Holy Spirit and it is sad that more people do not seek this gift. I believe that I understand those who reject it because I did the same, until I noticed how fruitful it is in the lives of others. My fear of looking foolish turned out to be a subtle form of pride. Today I rejoice in the gift of tongues. It helped overcome frustrations in prayer and taught me many fruitful lessons. Prayer should emanate from the heart. The key to prayer is not manufacturing words with our mind, but focusing the aspirations of the heart on the Lord. His throne is in our heart and from there he becomes Lord of our total life.

Praying in tongues is an effective school for learning how to yield to God's will. Everything in life requires a certain balance in order that things go well. When I play golf I often try too hard, and my golf game goes awry. A certain abandon is necessary for a good golf swing. When I go skiing, sometimes I try too hard. I constantly want to be under control and then the skiing does not go well. There is a certain abandon that is required to ski with the hill instead of against it—then skiing becomes fun and exhilarating. I believe the same is true with our prayer life. We have to learn that delicate abandon where we yield to our Father and we cooperate with him. It does not depend totally upon us and it does not depend totally upon him.

The spiritual life is a living partnership with Jesus so that he abides in us and we abide in him, and thus our life becomes fruitful. Learning to pray in tongues schools us in yielding to that partnership with the Lord. Tongues are a key to prayer, because the Holy Spirit is always supposed to be part of our prayer. We must learn when it depends upon us and when it depends upon him. Praying in tongues has made that clear and made prayer much easier.

Praying in tongues is also an advantage when we are filled with the desire to give praise to God but run out of words in a short time. This prayer in tongues allows the Spirit of God to make his groanings within our hearts. As they are expressed on our lips, we can enter into a much fuller praise. Our praise and thanksgiving become a greater part of us as we abandon ourselves to the Holy Spirit and let the words "bubble up" from within. These are the groanings of the Holy Spirit. He makes it easier to rejoice in the Lord always.

There are other occasions when we are asked to pray for intentions, and it is not at all clear to us what is the proper prayer. Should I pray that a person be restored to health, or that he or she will be given a peaceful death? Should I pray that this person will get the job he or she seeks and move away, or should I pray that he or she will find more happiness in the word that he or she now has? We are constantly confronted with people asking us to pray for petitions, and we do not know what God's holy will is for that person. I use the prayer of tongues when I feel uneasy about a prayer request. I do want to be a brother or sister to those who come to me with prayer intentions, and the Holy Spirit knows what the proper prayer is.

There are also times when prayer brings us close to ecstasy and we find ourselves in God's arms and want to be led by him. Sometimes silence seems appropriate and other times we want to express in song and word the wonders that God is performing within us. Praying in tongues, especially when sung, gives glory to God and brings one into deeper union with him. When a person is depressed because his or her life seems to be falling apart, praying in tongues often brings relief. Such chaotic moments can emerge from the subconscious and we cannot find words to express the unknown. By praying in tongues we allow the Holy Spirit to bring the hidden to light, and sometimes subconscious ills are healed. This kind of healing is only a personal theory of mine. I do know from personal experience and from counseling others that chaos can give way to peace by praying in tongues.

Praying in tongues can also be fruitful when we quietly pray in our hearts while listening to a teaching or a sermon. I cannot say that I know why, but I do know that it helps me discern what the Lord is trying to reveal through the teacher I am listening to. The fruits which flow from praying in tongues have led me to value the gift of tongues as a special grace of prayer.

The Scriptures tell us that we should "pray always," and this is a great challenge for the Christian. As I learn these new forms of prayer and try to live in the presence of God, faith in him colors the little things of every day. Jesus wants to be with me when I am driving my car, answering a telephone or doorbell, listening to a troubled person, or reading the paper. Everything I do can be prayer if I can take the time to be with him in personal prayer. As I learn to invite him to join me each day with all that is in it, including interruptions, I am discovering a new peace. We do have to learn to "pray always."

Prayer is not so much a matter of words as it is a matter of living in God's presence. We need to be in union with him, for without him we can do nothing. Many times during the day God is trying to reach us in very ordinary ways. We have to give him a chance to touch us, to come into our lives. We have to "inhale" his blessings—and this is prayer. At other times we should be responding with praise and thanks, petition or sorrow. When we reach out to him with expressions of faith, hope and love, when we hum or sing or reflect or just say "Praise the Lord," we are "exhaling." Prayer is the "breath of the spirit." "Come to me, all you who are weary and find life burdensome, and I will refresh you. Take my yoke upon your shoulders and learn from me, for I am gentle and humble of heart. Your souls will find rest, for my yoke is easy and my burden light" (Mt. 11:28-30). ●

"Lift up your hearts"

ROMEO BLANCHETTE

"Sursum Corda"—"Lift up your hearts"—is an exhortation to, and at the same time a definition of, prayer. In this brief dissertation concerning my personal prayer experience, I must begin by saying that the highest form of prayer is sacrifice, and the perfect sacrifice is holy Mass. For me to preside at Mass is to take the place of Christ himself—both priest and victim. It is difficult to describe this experience, but not difficult to recognize this sublime reality. It has always been with joy

and awe, penance and thanksgiving that for thirty-nine years I have said Mass acting as Christ did and at the same time representing him as leader of his people, his mystical body.

In administering the other mysteries of Christ, his sacraments, again the realization of bringing Christ to his people and his people to him has been a source of great inner sense of union with God. Truly my heart has been lifted to him.

In the recitation of the Divine Office, another public prayer of Christ's

---

Most Reverend Romeo Blanchette, D.D. is Bishop of Joliet.

11

Church, I have again, in spite of many distractions, been conscious of my role as mediator between men and God.

I imagine, however, that this article is meant more to dwell on my personal experience in private prayer. The story of the illiterate person who daily spent hours before the Blessed Sacrament has deeply affected me and my approach to prayer. As the story goes, someone finally approached this simple, humble man and asked him what he did during all this time. "I look at him and he looks at me" was his simple, yet deeply profound answer.

Another incident from first-hand knowledge that has made a profound impression on me in my attitude toward prayer is the following: Someone was dying of cancer, and the parish priest, who would bring him Communion frequently, asked him what he did all day, if he found time hanging heavily on his hands, and if he watched TV much of the time. The touching answer was, "I spend most of my time thinking about God and how good he is and how wonderful it will be to be with him in heaven."

These incidents of simple prayerful faith correspond pretty much to my experience in private prayer. I consider prayer a dialogue with God: I talk to him and he talks to me. Of course, in the quiet presence of the Blessed Sacrament, I am more conscious that Christ is there really and truly as he was in Palestine some 1,900 years ago. And as one of his apostles, I try to develop some of the familiarity that the original Twelve had with him. I come to him for strength in difficult times; I come to him for comfort in sad moments; I come to him for courage when things seem so bleak; and I come to him for help and wisdom in meeting particularly complicated situations and in trying to make wise decisions that seem so impossible at times.

When joyous moments such as a particularly effective encounter, conversation, talk or sermon have taken place, or when a sinner has come back to the fold, or when an innocent child has said "I love you," I come to him to share these joys and say "Thank you." When, reading and meditating on the Scriptures, I find a particular passage that draws me closer to Christ by relating to my daily life or my striving to be a better bishop to his and my flock, I have the joy of experiencing a closeness to him in my own personal life and work; this brings inner peace that is indescribable.

I find it very real—and not at all spectacular—to sense the very presence of God in my soul. At no time—at least, not for a long period of time—do I feel that God is not with me and ready to talk and offer his replies through the inspiration of his Holy Spirit if I simply pause to listen wherever I may be.

The daily habit of saying the rosary while walking or while driving a car (alone or with someone) has been mine for years. As I do this, in spite of distractions that come my way, I find it easy to imagine that Jesus and Mary are walking (or riding) with me as I relive their lives full of glory, joys, and sorrows. This daily habit—in my opinion—has made it possible to maintain my sanity when everything around me seemed inane, made it possible to maintain peace of mind when troubles seemed so to engulf me that Job's life seemed really my own, and made it possible to maintain an attempt to be forgiving when apparent injustice seemed to be overwhelming me. This devotion to the rosary, together with devotion to the Sacred Heart and a sense of the abiding presence of the Holy Spirit, has made unspoken spontaneous prayer relatively easy—but absolutely necessary in trying to serve God conscientiously, and in trying to make every action of a very busy life a prayer. I have not always succeeded, but even the failures I try to make prayerful by telling God of my weaknesses and inadequacies. And I hear him say, "I understand, my son; be not afraid; lift up your heart!" ●

"Prayer is the choreography, the poetry, the symphony of existence"

AIDAN KAVANAGH

It quite escapes me why anyone would be interested in my own personal experience of prayer. Anecdotes about this would either bore others (like wallet snapshots) or tell analysts more about me than I care to have them know. I interview badly lying down. Worse, a large part of my adult life has been spent avoiding the issue or retreating in confusion before systematized techniques for praying "well." The Spiritual Exercises of Ignatius frighten the wits out of me; charismatics who breathe their own prayer life on my neck embarrass me speechless. People who discourse about prayer easily and well (or even badly, for that matter) fill me with awe. They also cause me to head toward the nearest door.

Whether this makes me a whited sepulchre is a question for debate. But pray I do—rather as I would talk to someone out of necessity because he is sitting next to me in the car or across from me at dinner. I talk because someone is there. I pray for the same reason. I talk because I am. I am because a whole vast array of presences intersect at a particular point. The point is I, and not all the intersecting presences are of this world. To some I talk, to the rest I pray. The discourses are what I am.

It is no big deal—in the same sense our Lord had in mind when he said the Kingdom is like a mustard seed or a bit of yeast. What I am is in itself as insignificant as a small seed or a spore of yeast. Whatever meaning we may have is inscrutable to the three of us. To discover the value of the seed, Jesus implies, one should inquire of the birds of the air (Mt. 13:31-32); to detect the spore's importance, ask those who eat the bread (Mt. 13:33); to lay bare the role of prayer in my life, examine my colleagues in faith.

Although I am unable to articulate adequately what prayer is in my own life, I may be able to describe the place in which the presences with whom I speak and to whom I pray seem to place me. An arithmetical formula may state it most clearly: $7 \times 7 + 1 = 50$.

This old Judaeo-Christian formula, because it defines the sort of creation in which man lives, describes the locale in which I pray. What the formula precisely denies is that where I pray is a place set apart from and in opposition to the rest of creation. The closet into

which I withdraw to pray is not a place of singular privacy but one of a peculiar intensity of presences: it is less a vault of concrete and steel than a glass-sided telephone booth set in the middle of Times Square, and the lines are all party lines. The formula affirms that seven—the digital symbol of all reality—is neither sacred nor secular but comprises six units of secular utility given shape and meaning by a seventh unit of sacral rest and non-utilitarian sabbatical festivity. God and labor unions agree on this.

But the formula goes much further when it multiplies the digital symbol of reality by itself—squares it—and then adds to this a sabbath of sabbaths which both consummates and exhausts all secularity as well as all sacrality in itself. The symbiosis of sabbath and workday, of feast and feria, of non-useful and useful, of sacred and secular, is transmuted into a new time that Jesus called the Kingdom. This is a third dimension of reality hinted at only weakly by sacred sabbath and secular feria. It is creation verging on its uncreated origin, the leaf becoming tap root, nature transmuting into grace in the person of him who is both man and uncreated Word existing evermore as a people riddled with his wounds as well as his unspeakable glory.

These are the Presences with whom I speak and pray because their intersections constitute and name who I am. I am their commerce; my speech and prayer are their discourse. Prayer is not an act; it is a state of being even more than the dance is not its steps, the poem its words, or the music its tones. Prayer is the choreography, the poetry, the symphony of existence raised in Christ to its sabbatical consummation in a cosmic liturgy that has no dismissal

Aidan Kavanagh, O.S.B., S.T.D. is presently acting director of the Yale Institute of Sacred Music.

for it has no end. The altar at which I pray is the body of the Church in Christ now standing like a lamb slain before the Father amid rolling crowns and beasts with many eyes.

My closet is an awful place. It is filled with children, wrestlers, blood, flowers, screams and hymns; dancers rocket through, martyrs burn, plumbers hammer, the telephone rings constantly while lovers moan and somebody practices on the cello in the corner. There is water on the floor, bread and wine on the table, spaghetti on the stove, and crosses stuck in all our hearts.

But for all this confusion the view is priceless, and fifty is the perfect age. ●

"My God, my God, why have you forsaken me?"

BERNARD J. TOPEL

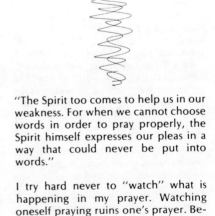

Several years ago, I was asked by *New Catholic World* to write an article—an article on my personal prayer, fasting, and almsgiving. I wrote it. I have again been asked by *New Catholic World* to write about my personal prayer. My first inclination was to decline. I wondered how I could write on this subject without being too repetitious. Then it occurred to me that it might be helpful —and not objectionably repetitious— to write on the difference between my prayer now and when I wrote the other article.

There is growth in prayer—unmistakably. Something would be wrong if there were not. Growth means change. There has been change in my prayer. "My" prayer? Not really mine. It has come to be the Holy Spirit's! I think of what St. Paul wrote to the Romans:

Most Reverend Bernard J. Topel, D.D. is Bishop of Spokane.

"The Spirit too comes to help us in our weakness. For when we cannot choose words in order to pray properly, the Spirit himself expresses our pleas in a way that could never be put into words."

I try hard never to "watch" what is happening in my prayer. Watching oneself praying ruins one's prayer. Besides, watching my prayer is not my job; it is the job of my spiritual director. He does it well.

Nor do I look back on my prayer, except when it seems necessary in order to help my spiritual director know what is happening in it. Consequently, there are limits to how much I remember about my prayer. However, I probably remember enough.

In these last few years, there has been in my prayer a great increase in living the paschal mystery—in living out Christ's suffering, death, and resurrection. I am not referring to living the paschal mystery by contemplating Christ's suffering, death, and resurrection prayerfully. Rather, I am speaking of a true suffering, dying, and rising within me in prayer. I had not expected this. I had always thought of my living the paschal mystery as on the outside of me. Now I know that my most important living of the paschal mystery is in my prayer.

"Suffering" in my prayer? There is. More than before. There is now more and deeper emptiness in my prayer. There is greater desolation than before —when God seems to be gone, gone completely and forever. There are times when I can rightly think of the words of the psalmist: "How long, O Lord, will you utterly forget me? How long will you hide your face from me?" Or I can think of the words of our Lord in the garden: "If you are willing, take this cup away from me. Nevertheless, let your will be done, not mine." Or think of our Lord's words on the cross: "My God, my God, why have you forsaken me?" Yes, I can rightly think of these while I know how insignificant is my desolation compared to his.

There is also a "dying" in my prayer. A dying to worldly things and desires. A dying experienced in a total helplessness. A being powerless to pray—and powerless elsewhere too! There is

dying too in the realization of my "nothingness." The powerlessness that I experience in my prayer is God's way of teaching me my powerlessness to do anything that really matters, to do anything that is really consequential to him. There is, then, growth in the realization that "all life, all holiness, comes from the Father, through Jesus Christ, by the working of the Holy Spirit," and not by my efforts. It is in this kind of prayer that God has really taught me my spiritual helplessness, has taught me that all the increase is his—every single bit of it. It was necessary, and a very great blessing, that I was taught this by him. It was, in fact, a wonderful demonstration of his love for me.

Two years ago, I used to think that God sometimes used me as his instrument. I no longer think that! Now I see my role to be at best an occasion for the Holy Spirit's action.

There is also a "resurrection" in my prayer. The "rising" comes from God being present within me in a deep and full and wonderfully loving way. It is a true "experiencing" of his love—of being loved and loving in return, with love that is far beyond any other love I have ever had or experienced.

There is also the marvelous gift of the Holy Spirit and all that his coming brings: greater insights, more spiritual certainty, stronger convictions, much deeper realization of spiritual truths. There is, as I have indicated, a greater realization of his presence and his love, and a greater power to love him in return. This last, I think, is the heart of the "resurrection" in my prayer.

One of the most important things the Holy Spirit has done for me in prayer is to give me the right and power to say

"Father" and to mean it when I say it. He has deepened my "understanding" of the Fatherhood of God, deepened my realization of how truly God is my Father, so that there is an "experiencing" too of his Fatherhood. I have found it an extremely important "experiencing."

St. Paul told the Galatians: "The proof that you are sons is that God has sent the Spirit of his Son into your hearts: the Spirit that cries, 'Abba Father,' and it is this that makes you a son." Certain it is, therefore, that "by the working of the Holy Spirit" I became a son of the Father, and have recognized this momentous truth. It is by him too, especially during prayer, that the realization that God is my Father has grown, and that all the glorious implications of that truth have also grown.

Through prayer, I see God's loving goodness to me as never before. I have been helped to be more grateful than before—more grateful by far. I have been helped to regret with a very great regret my failures to be grateful to him. I see much more accurately the magnitude of his love for me. There is, then, much more trust and confidence on my part. It is, consequently, with great confidence that I say to him at Mass: "Protect us from all anxiety." Over and over and over again the Holy Spirit makes clear to me that God is my most loving Father. The Father shows his love for me in literally everything that happens. It is, however, in prayer that I see this most of all.

My spiritual helplessness does not worry me—not in the least! The love of my Father for me is enough—far more than enough. The weaker I know myself to be, and the weaker I am, the more he loves me. These convictions,

and many more, are given to me by the Holy Spirit in prayer.

The most significant book I read just prior to the Council was Durrwell's *The Resurrection.* Its impact on me was very great, as was its impact on the whole Church. The comparison of a funeral now with one twenty years ago gives proof of that statement.

Durrwell also wrote a book entitled *In the Redeeming Christ.* He dedicated it to the Blessed Mother and to the saint "who has been the humblest and certainly the best spiritual writer in our own time." Guess who? St. Thérèse of Lisieux! The heart of her spiritual doctrine was the Fatherhood of God and our spiritual childhood. She carried it to its logical conclusions, to complete trust and total abandonment and entire confidence in the love of the Father. All this was rooted in a burning faith and a consuming love.

It has been years since I have read much from St. Thérèse. I remember enough, though, to realize that something of her spirit and experience and love has been given to me in prayer. I thank God for that. It is so certainly not my work. It is the "working of the Holy Spirit" in me.

The Holy Spirit, then, in prayer gives me exceedingly important convictions and realizations and insights. He gives me something else of even more importance—love. He is the Spirit of love. He gives us the Lord's kind of love—a love that is very different from most other love.

St. Paul's description to the Corinthians of that love tells us how different it is. That kind of love is "always patient and kind; it is never jealous or conceited, it is never selfish, it does not take offense, and is not resentful; it is always ready to excuse, to trust, to hope, and to endure whatever comes. It is a love that does not come to an end."

We need to grow in this kind of love. Christ gave us a commandment to that effect. He called it the "new commandment." In the second Eucharistic Prayer we beg God to "make us grow in love"—"grow" in his kind of love. When such love is given to us, we recognize how accurate is St. Paul's description of it. We recognize how different it is from the way we usually love, and how powerless—how totally powerless—we are to get it by ourselves. No wonder, for this is Christ's kind of love—the kind of love that the Father has for his Son. That is exactly what Jesus said of it.

Such love is a gift, a pure gift. St. Paul told the Romans that it is "poured out in our hearts by the Holy Spirit." He pours this love into our hearts especially in and through prayer. When he does, one comes to know (as St. Paul says) "the love of Christ which is beyond all knowledge," and to have "God's own peace, which is beyond all understanding." One comes to possess his joy too!

More clearly than before I see that my prayer reaches its summit in the Eucharist, provided that my celebration of the Eucharist is preceded by sufficient prayerful reflection, and preceded too by asking the Holy Spirit's help, and Mary's powerful intercession, to pray the Eucharist as well.

Small wonder that the Eucharist should be the summit of prayer. For at Mass, the death and resurrection of Jesus (the paschal mystery) are made actually present. Further, there is no better way to give thanks to the Father "always and everywhere" than through Jesus Christ in the Eucharist.

Moreover, the Eucharist is truly the sacrament of love. Its purpose is to unite us with Jesus in a thrilling union of love that makes us one with him—and thereby one with each other. It is no exaggeration to say that the Eucharist, and the Eucharistic prayer, can —and should—transform us into Christ through love. All this and so much more besides come to us in the Eucharist "by the working of the Holy Spirit."

Our Father loves us far more than we know. Because he loves us so much, he wants our Lord's love, peace, joy—and much more besides—to be ours. If we do our part—especially in prayer— they will be!

Prayer? Its importance? Its power? Words of St. Paul come to my mind: "Glory be to him whose power working in us can do infinitely more than we can ask or imagine."

This power I now find in prayer! ●

DOROTHY H. DONNELLY

"This lover is faithful."

"Be careful, you'll spill it and burn the house down!" My sister, Rose, straightened out the Sacred Heart oil-lamp in my numb fingers before its wick-flame ignited the book and the bed we were sharing in a forbidden after-lights-out reading binge in our big old house in San Francisco. We vainly hoped my mother wouldn't see light from a vigil-lamp under the door!

Dorothy H. Donnelly, C.S.J. holds a Th.D. from Graduate Theological Union, Berkeley, and is presently director of spirituality on the faculty of the Pacific School of Religion.

The book had nothing to do with prayer—yet—but the lamp says much to me about the enclosing warmth of the deep faith of my Dad and Mom. Faith and prayer were our atmosphere, never separated from our woes, worries, joys, all expressed with appropriate Gaelic sentiment upon each occasion—the prayer of "exclamation" was never foreign to us. My father used the direct method. I can still hear his tread in the hall and his knock on our bedroom door every First Friday morning: "OK, girls, it's 6 o'clock!" And off we went to the 6:30 at Salesian Corpus

Christi in the outer Mission—and nobody minded, because he went, too.

Confession each month before First Friday went like clockwork, everybody trooping, class after class, to church with no thought of our "regimentation." In fact, we enjoyed the break from classes. I especially loved it because of my confessor, a beautiful old Salesian whose broken Italian-English and talented musical background translated my name, "Dorothy Donnelly" into "Hello, Doro-tee Do-re-mi" as he slid back the screen and we chatted on and on as I told him my monthly horrenda—always to a kindly ear.

Those Catholic school years introduced me to St. Joseph (our sisters were from Orange, California) and to St. John Bosco, so much livelier than St. Joseph somehow, battling in the streets of Turin for his ragged boys. Besides he did magic tricks—a new idea for a saint, one greatly augmented by my later introduction to Thomas More in eighth grade. He had brains, besides, and told jokes, even climbing scaffolds! I fell promptly in love and never got over it, devouring biographies with a passion that resulted one day in a doctoral thesis.

But the lady who added the "prayer" dimension to faith and courage was that spunky little consumptive, Marie-Thérèse Martin, dashing off to Rome to get the Pope to open Carmel. Last summer as our train sped past the sunny walls of her basilica in Lisieux I could only marvel how deeply and how long that demure, steely-soft sister of mine had challenged me to try to grow. Her "Story of a Soul" was my bible, and I imbibed her ways to pray, to see God, even how she thought about sickness and death.

By the end of high school, however, she had to retire to Carmel for sure as I decided to experience the world: work, friends, social life, dating, and even study. A year later, to my real surprise (but not that of Tess, Joe, or Tom More), I did enter Orange after telling the sisters no. On the way downstairs from that negative, I was caught by the far-flung panorama of San Francisco-out-the-window—and the sight of a blossoming cherry in one of its secret hanging gardens—and suddenly I knew that I had to "try it" if even for two weeks. I suppose they are still recovering from that quick reversal. The two weeks have been quite long.

Little "Tess" and Tom More had taught me that Christian life was heroic, exciting, and hard, too, so convent meditation (sweating out the Southern California summer hands deep in big black sleeves) was a way to get through to God by "thinking straight ahead." Fortunately my emotional side woke up, too, and I found prayer, saints, perfection bathed in a warm glow. I was a novice who never quite understood what everybody was doing, but enjoyed most of it still. Though Scripture was not part of our training I somehow got to final vows deeply in love with the psalms, those heart-openers that saved me from the "points" of meditation. Luckily, my novice mistress was a holy lady so the methodology didn't matter.

Once out, I taught and taught and taught, loving every minute of it, finding daily meditation a place to stop, breathe, often sleep, but at least be quiet, and "spiritual reading" each day was the source of whatever spiritual growth took place. Study, too (on the side!), was always pressing, so three degrees and some years later, death suddenly challenged my values and called for a reassessment. I lost my father and sister within two years, took off to the G.T.U. for a sabbatical to see if theology had any explanation, for my head needed to understand, too. Instead, I discovered Protestant theology, ecumenical joy, and, when I began to teach it myself, a great expansion of my horizons that demanded rethinking. Meanwhile the stress of change and another degree led me back to Scripture for my prayer. The Spirit truly woke up my heart, and with Fr. Don Gelpi's theology courses, many pieces came together to combine the intellectual and emotional phases of growth. My own teaching, especially co-teaching with him, and the writing that seemed to grow from it naturally—all of it poured power into my prayer which became communion with a dear friend who didn't worry about sin, lapses, errors, foolishness, but who demanded total surrender.

From my patristic studies, Gregory of Nyssa had shown me a great reverence for Scripture. Before opening that book, I learned to ask its true author, the Spirit, to teach me what he wanted me to learn that day. The Scripture is now my springboard for prayer. I needed to decide to take time strictly each day for God's Spirit to give me the serenity and vision needed for meaning to touch my life.

So after *deciding* to take time to pray, then *taking time* comes next, keeping that appointment with Truth each day to listen, be attentive and to wait and wait and wait, for we don't pray to have God hear us, but that we will hear God. But, then, to stop when God touches my heart and to go with God in joy, love, tears, aspirations, little cries of the heart in praise, thanks, adoring this One who has come so tenderly, molding us from within (Rom. 12).

Out of this going with God come peace, joy, and trust that make life exciting, light-some. I no longer need to use good energy wondering about my "perfection," a useless trip. No, rather there is a breathless daily agenda God gives us in prayer. Sins, mistakes, faults, yes, are a real cause for regret and we work to get rid of them, but how differently! No panic, shock, refusal to try again because the great "I" could sin or be wrong! Of course! Now everything is "of course," when we let the Spirit in.

The wonder was: What was I beating my head in about, when all the time the content of prayer comes from God? I don't supply it, only the time, only myself present and aware, listening, only myself letting go to God. If I can't let go, I ask God for letting-go as a gift God wants me to have in Jesus' name: the gift of let-go-ness. Sometimes, even, I let go of "praying" when it can become an idol or something I tend to own and I just go where God calls in our time together, as God pleases, to go with the river—and stop scrubbing the raft.

No, I don't know who this God is in my prayer, but I know a bit more than I did. Never will I catch God in my butterfly net or that's not my God! But gradually this "great sneak" of a God moved into my space, always initiating love, pain, questions, enticing me into the growth-pattern God desires. He is also the "great pedagogue" of Clement of Alexandria, the ultimate teacher whom I now want to teach me, to hear, even to follow, no matter how much I fear change simply because I now know that this is the God who spends his non-time giving himself away, a God who will accept only one compliment—trust—and who pulls a corresponding trust from me. This God is a giver of gifts: the Son, the Spirit, and my very self and all the selves about me. I know that God wants in return my trust and love because trusting him means I believe that this lover is faithful, and that is his name.●

"Not everyone who says Lord, Lord..."

JOSEPH P. WHELAN

A thousand words or so, the invitation said, about my "personal prayer experience." I take acceptance as a covenant with all who read these words to be as honest as I can. But reticence is not excluded by this promise. There is a reverence, a silence, owed to any relationship when telling others of it.

A thousand words. Far too many, for

Joseph P. Whelan, S.J., Ph.D. is director of Jesuits in Training, Maryland Province.

something words will never manage, even badly. Impossibly too few, even to sketch its general shape, given the variety of his times and ways. And so it is tempting to temporize, defensively, in the face of words, words asking about something at once so awful and so simple; so detailed, and yet empty; something precious that is so often tawdry, idolatrous, domesticated, used; something I reject outright, often; something so dark, so increasingly dark, so uncomforting and, at its best, apparently so uninformative, yet something which, when done, done *in* me, *for* me, often chooses and centers my journey, now blessing now judging the search and the act, sometimes lighting, *often* lighting, even delighting, with its darkness, my days.

Something? Someone. Someone whose holiness is as warmly, humanly available as Jesus' love of friends; and as decisive as Jesus' anger in the cleansing of the temple; and as clear as Jesus' blunt, imperative self-portrait in Matthew 25. Someone whose love and mercy are also intransigent holiness, vivid, silent mystery; totally near in Jesus; but, like Jacob with the angel, *more* mysterious for having come so near: Mystery very near, yet inaccessible and terrible as how there may be leukemia or starving among children, or how Gethsemane may be asked of the innocence of Jesus; as inaccessible and beautiful as how I am to live at all before him in this world according to the ethic of the eight Beatitudes. But Someone too whose holiness, perfectly passed over into Jesus' weakness, is powerful forever now of that joyous Easter call—that Father's call, Lover's call, that call of *God* to all, across all history, who so much as touch on even the hem of the garment of Christ's yes: "Come, my beloved, my lovely one, come." Mystery.

But also, mission. For the call is also, even more so: "Go, into the whole world, to the very ends of the earth." Mystery—and mission. Both are *internal* to the wholly Trinitarian reality of valid prayer, as I am finding it. And they are internal to it only in their character as *internal to each other*, which is the lever by which prayer escapes itself, becoming action, and by which action keeps faithful to its destiny as reverent, servant love. Mystery as mis-

sionary: he is a missionary God, incarnational, worldly, a companion for the road. Mission as mysterious: action in the world, with all its density, distraction and detail, its celebration and fatigue, is the preferred place and time for adoration, however dark. Finding all things in God, and God in all things.

The experience is one of much distraction, frequent absence—mine, not his; steady fidelity—his, not mine; intimacy and distance—mutual. The struggle is not especially to *do* anything—he does that—but to be present, to be *there*. It took long years to learn, just a little, that what is interesting is not prayer—much less meditation, or its techniques—but *God*. Prayer is only derivatively interesting, but it is enormously interesting, because *he* is. And the world is interesting, because it is what is on his mind, in his heart. The world from his point of view: *there's* the agony that is worth all tears, the beautiful reality worth all gratitude, the exciting future worth all strength. For the world, especially its people—it is all Jesus, the full, entire Jesus whom the Father seeks to say, strives to do.

Without prayer, I lose all this. It goes opaque, gets notional. Or it gets grabbed at, stridently, instead of coming to me, as a gift to see and do. And the demonic—largely, though not entirely, a big word for me in my selfishness—makes it tricky, when it is not simply boring, slovenly routine. Demonic, because all, all creation is potentially Jesus. But in any, in every given choice, and in the actions that give flesh and history to choice, there is smashing of idols to be done. "Not everyone who says, Lord, Lord . . ." "If anyone says to you, 'Look, here is Christ!' or 'There he is!' don't believe it." No. There is listening, thanking, begging, searching, finding, confirming to do. All this in presence to the Father, as Ignatius Loyola prayed, that *he* may place us with the Son—with the corporate, contemporary, suffering, worldly Jesus carrying his cross. Searching, finding, thanking to do, as Jesus constantly did, and does—in the temptations, for example, or when sufficient bread was lacking. Discerning to *do*? To *accept*, as gift for the doing. All, all is grace. Even the asking, the searching. Especially the suffering, the praise.

I pray often, regularly—I hope such information is what's wanted—forty to fifty minutes, perhaps five times a week; and then, three or four times a day, two to five minutes of explicit recollection—of remembering, collecting, asking to be *there*; and I look to be given other brief moments of begging, thanking, complaining, anger, or whatever; and also, usually something at night. Adoration, I find, most frequently given. And best. Because while it may, it doesn't *need* to, understand, grieve, enjoy, or judge. Just believe.

Just believe! My life, my prayer—my prayer because my life—is filled with unbelief, and its cold consequence: compensations. Usually it starts with loss of gratitude, which is to lose humility. And then the real if undramatic moving into fears—and so to the falling back on, and the seeking out of, self. The time given to prayer, as described above, is therefore not impressive, or certainly would not be thought so, if the much-tried alternatives were spelled out here.

Nevertheless, over recent years I think I have been taught, despite the infidelities, that the life he does in me is fundamentally stronger than the death I do. I have therefore dared to ask not to entertain a systematic doubt about myself—my thoughts, my instincts, or desires—as if, on principle, his looks and hopes were elsewhere—granting any given instance might be an exception. Rather I have felt invited to initial trust and affirmation—and looking for thanksgiving—a trust however which, because of well-attested weakness, sinfulness, lack of recollection, certainly requires testing, blessing, denial, or whatever, in the companionship of prayer.

What do I do, what happens, at least often, in my regular, more lengthy experiences of prayer? I use Scripture, most often. And if not that, usually nothing. Interesting: it is extremely rare that any Scripture passage is really available unless it has been given to me previously, whether in my hearing it or my reading it aloud, with *others*—be the sharing with a single friend, or within a large and formal liturgy. In this most important sense, I am never alone with God in prayer. And in another sense too: I find small difference in the *at once* essentially social, essentially solitary, character of my prayer—*if* I am really praying—whether I am alone in my room or participating in, or leading, a large liturgy. The experiences are very different, but not in their social, solitary character. Of course the unjust aspects of my life and action and of my moral sensibility deeply affect the social character of my prayer. But they affect the solitude as well. For the issue there is not solitude, but solipsism.

In the prayer itself, Jesus is there—often felt, sighted, heard, at the start. Not always, or even *very* often. But often. And then, usually, and soon, he stills, darkens (lightens?), to a presence that is—apperceptive? Anyway, a presence that is not, cannot, be focused. Much begging, much thanking—sometimes with words, sometimes without them—up to this point. And then? I don't know. I do not know. Except that it is the Father. And—no trace of doubt—that it is *Jesus'* Father. Nothing seen. Nothing heard. Sometimes, touches—his, not mine. Touch: obviously an image, but I cannot do better. And then, when he gives it: wonderful, freeing extroversion. Adoration. Extroversion into him. And at the end sometimes, but more often only later, during the day, or during the days ahead, extroversion into Jesus once again. Jesus: occasionally given to be *found*, in the persons, issues, "busy work" of my life; or, more often, Jesus given to be *searched for*, given to be *done*. The experience is never glamorous, certainly never psychologically odd. Peaceful. Energizing. Scouring.

Mostly desert, darkness, endurance. Difficult. But never *really* painful. Not the passion. It's no false modesty to say I have not learned the obedience, or the poverty, for that adventure.

One more, final fact. The decade has seen Mary largely fade from my prayer. But this is now well past. I have recovered her, been given her again, in remembering what an aging brother Jesuit said to me long ago: "They have no wine. . . . They don't know how to pray. Do whatever he tells you. Well, when you pray, say: Father."

It is not satisfying to have sketched what is above—as if there were "typical" prayer. *I* may be that. But a typical God? Well. More than a thousand words. Yet, fragments. Without closure. Stop. ●

"For you, I am a bishop; with you, I am a Christian"

JOHN F. WHEALON

With no enthusiasm have I accepted the invitation from *New Catholic World* to write about personal prayer experiences. Personal prayer is personal and should remain personal.

But I have long felt that we Catholics are overly reticent about our personal prayer. The struggles and failures, the fumblings and bumblings of each of us can be of genuine help to others.

Most Reverend John F. Whealon, D.D., S.S.L. is Archbishop of Hartford.

Ideally every parish is a community of prayer where techniques of personal prayer are regularly taught to parishioners. But we have hardly started to move toward that ideal. Any techniques of prayer being taught these days are, it seems, taught outside the parish family. We Catholics, heirs of a magnificent prayer tradition, should speak more of our Catholic prayer tradition and of our own experience in praying.

Prayer is of course a gift from God—a

gift for which we dispose ourselves—and when it comes to prayer, we are all amateurs. In public or liturgical prayer—the Mass and the Divine Office—a priest or bishop or deacon carries a special role and responsibility. But our fundamental prayer is private prayer—that kind of prayer which our Lord once described as closing the door of our room and praying in secret to our heavenly Father. And the door of a Catholic bishop's room is no different from the door of a lay Catholic's room. Our private prayer is the same. As St. Augustine said of himself: "For you, I am a bishop; with you, I am a Christian."

My prayer life and vocation were strongly influenced by my parents. There was no family prayer (apart from prayers at meals) in those pre-Peyton days. But both parents attended daily Mass whenever possible. My father, an overworked optometrist, ended every day with the private recitation of the rosary in the living room. My mother, as I learned after her death, said the Stations of the Cross twice each day. Children of such rare parents should know something about prayer.

At the age of thirteen I entered the oldest minor seminary in the nation, St. Charles College in Catonsville, Maryland. There the Sulpician Fathers handed on a way of living and praying that went back unchanged from seventeenth-century French Catholicism. It was all quite tough and disciplined—the "grand silence" from night prayers until after breakfast, the rising at 5:45 A.M., morning prayers and meditation (Sulpician method with a spiritual bouquet) at 6:15 A.M. before the Community Mass. The liturgy—solemn Latin Masses, Sunday vespers, Gregori-

an Chant—was magnificent though impersonal.

For twelve formative seminary years I was formed according to that pattern of pre-Mass meditation, daily Scripture reading, daily rosary, daily spiritual reading.

Now thirty-one years have passed since ordination. What surprises me is that, while so much has changed, so much has remained and has even become more meaningful.

I don't know what benefits came from all those hours of morning meditations. There must have been benefits—advances in eliminating faults and in Christlike living. But the benefits were not measurable. The idea, however, of preserving sacrosanct a half-hour before Mass (or breakfast) has continued. I rise an hour before morning Mass, refuse on principle to turn on the radio or TV, and hold that early hour as the day's first fruits to be spent in minimally distracted prayer. The example of Fathers Gleason, Saupin and Klaphecke, disciplined old-time Sulpicians, perdures in this life of their student.

The Mass? It means much more now. I loved the old Latin Mass, the Gregorian Chant, the exact rubrics. But the new form of Mass is to me more spiritual, more biblical, closer to Christ. I still celebrate in Latin at least once a week, so as to hold on to a dear Catholic and personal tradition.

The Divine Office or Breviary has changed much. It used to be a chore, monotonous and time consuming—a sheer duty offered each day to God. Now it is much shorter: for me five minutes after Mass for morning prayer; three minutes at noon for daytime prayer; ten minutes before dinner for evening prayer and the office of readings; two minutes before retiring for night prayer. It is a normal part of the day's operations—an easy, pleasant prayer, in harmony with the liturgical cycle and the Church universal.

I have tried to practice—and have preached to others—a pattern of adult morning prayers. The recommendation is to say them after washing and dressing. Then kneel or sit down before a crucifix. Greet and praise God (e.g., the "Glory Be"); thank God for life and the good people on whose shoulders we stand; make an act of faith (I believe in God and in the way of Christ); an act of hope (I trust in God and not in this world or government or humans or myself); an act of love (I will return love to God and all God's children). It takes only a few minutes and is a proper start to the day.

The rosary has always been a problem. It calls for an unrushed, contemplative approach—and rarely have I been adequate to the rosary. I have developed a short rosary—saying ten times (on the first decade) "Hail, Mary, full of grace, the Lord is with you," and then ten times on subsequent decades: "Blessed are you among women," "Blessed is the fruit of your womb, Jesus," "Holy Mary, Mother of God, pray for us sinners," "Pray now and at the hour of our death. Amen." I see the rosary as important, as wanted by the Blessed Mother, as especially devotional for October and May. I am grateful for the short rosary on those

days when I am rushed—and that is most days.

The two books that have helped most to date have been Leen's *Progress in Mental Prayer* and Archbishop Anthony Bloom's *Learning To Pray*. For each morning meditation I have written down thoughts in a notebook and have filled dozens of notebooks. I recently made a Marriage Encounter and found that this is part of the Encounter technique of communication.

But now I am finding that this pattern of meditation is repetitious, somehow no longer appropriate. There is a realization that something more direct and less intellectual is the adventure ahead —that I should be relating to God without all this thinking and cerebral exercising and daily attempt to inform external wisdom. It has been most helpful to learn from the Trappist monks at Spencer that contemplation should lie shortly beyond meditation, and that there is a method of contemplation—the prayer of centering— that goes back to the fourteenth-century book *The Cloud of Unknowing*. This method is easily taught and can be learned from a cassette tape available at the St. Joseph Abbey Gift Shop in Spencer, Massachusetts. It means putting the intellect into idle gear so as to contemplate God more intimately.

Where all this will lead I do not know. But prayer life is ultimately the real life, the link with God. As the chambered nautilus seals off one chamber and moves into a new one, so I hope to be somehow making progress in prayer with the passing of the years.●

"In the presence of God my Mother"

ARLENE SWIDLER

I suspect most Catholics looking back at their prayer life over the past ten years tend to be swamped with pessimism. Although we are grateful for the good things Vatican II brought us, we Catholics also suffer today from a lack of community, a lingering distrust of lay for clergy and clergy for laity, a boredom with a not very spectacular

Ms. Arlene Swidler is editor of *Journal of Ecumenical Studies*.

English liturgy and—more especially for women—frustration, a sense of being deliberately humiliated, sudden spurts of rage, and, too often, a not-quite-conscious fear that the powers of evil may be too firmly entrenched in the Church to allow any hope. It all adds up to a spiritual restlessness that sometimes makes proceeding much beyond the mere desire to pray impossible, a restlessness that is the opposite of St. Augustine's restlessness of the heart seeking God. But, because it springs at bottom from a love for the Church, I for one can't reject the pain. So it's a miserable situation.

Sometimes I try going back. This summer I secretly returned to my rosary to see whether there had been something in its rhythms that would still satisfy my spiritual needs. It didn't work. On the other hand, when my husband and I say monastic Compline together—in Latin, I must confess, and not often—we find it right.

However the two things that bring me most joy in prayer would also not have been possible without all the changes of the past decade, and perhaps I am lacking in gratitude in dwelling on the pain the Church's growth has brought us.

The first is a family thing—we're part of the ecumenical movement. Without conscious planning, we've made it a ritual that during Lent and Advent we attend services in another church once a week. Not that praying in other confessions is a penance, but it does involve planning ahead and adjusting schedules. Occasionally we use this time to attend a Jewish sabbath service or a Quaker first-day meeting or an Eastern Orthodox liturgy; often we simply accept the ministries of music offered by Protestant congregations and experience Elgar's "Dream of Gerontius" or Rossini's "Stabat Mater." Lent and Advent seem a good time to be open to God in new manifestations and to build a few fragile ties in the network of the universal human family. Our little pilgrimages bring an interior alertness to us; afterward there's often something to share together in meditation or conversation.

My second innovation is far more complex to talk about. In brief, I find that retiring to my room at a quiet hour, sitting in a modified lotus position and putting myself in the presence of God who is my Mother is the most relaxing and most invigorating spiritual experience I know.

How I arrived at this style is clear enough. Many of us women over the past decades have begun by questioning antiquated Church laws, moved to criticizing contemporary Church practice and theology, and then confronted our notion of God. We saw how by believing that the male Adam was made in the image of God we had formulated a God in the image of the male. The male God is more pervasive than we realize; not long ago my talk at a state college was interrupted by a freshman who said, "Did you hear what you just said? 'Of course God's not male or female; he's neither.'" The unexpected tensions that arise when we suggest using female language for God in the Mass show how deeply the Father God has encroached on the feminine aspects of divine personhood.

Fortunately scholarship over the past years has pointed out often enough that both the Old Testament and the New use feminine imagery for God and that even Jesus pictured God as a woman in the parable of the lost coin. Clearly he didn't mean God is female; the woman is just a figure of speech, and that's what God as Father or Mother is.

Nevertheless, I did hesitate over the propriety of such prayer, as many women hesitate. Will my praying to God my Mother introduce still more divisiveness into the Church? Is God as Mother a concept I can expect of all

God's children, or just a private gimmick? Do we pray to the living personal God as *neither* male nor female or as *both* female and male? I decided that as long as we humans still identify ourselves strongly as female or male we must include both in our address to God, and that attendance at Mass over the decades has given me a strong attachment for God my Father which praying to God my Mother will not counterbalance for a long long time.

St. Joan's Alliance has a kind of unofficial motto going back to its founding before the First World War: "We are feminist because we are Catholic." As an expression of the Christian message it's good; people understand it and respond to it. But I don't think many of us would formulate it that way today. Our primary knowledge of God comes from experience, and my knowledge of God as Mother precedes my membership in the Church. It is not a secondary or peripheral matter.

Being in the presence of God my Mother does not involve a discursive thought process. One is simply there. I am aware that the word Mother refers to nothing new: simply God as my creator and shaper, that which supports me always, source of wisdom and grace. Yet when I consider how she lives in me and I live in her, how the world is hers, and how her image is seen in all of us, I find myself healing, becoming whole once again. I learn nothing new, and yet all is renewed. Although I have always known I am made in the image of God, it is now all of me, down to the gestures of my fingertips, that shares in the divine reflection. Although I have always recognized God's grace in me, there are special hidden corners and nooks deep down where I can now sense God my Mother. And although my sense of mission has long been strong, seeing the world as God my Mother's collapses all the responsibility-barriers our sexist culture has set up.

In the presence of God my Mother, life becomes simple once again. But right now the insight is only fragmentary and fleeting. ●

"Was it not ordained that Christ should suffer and so enter into his glory?"

MARGARET BRENNAN

Because prayer for me is above all a "response-ability" to God, my own experience has grown and changed and nuanced with that same growth and change in myself, especially during the past decade.

The profound changes in the Church's understanding of its own life and mission, the emerging humanization in our relationships to one another, and the growing sense of responsibility for the lifting of burdens of oppression in the pursuance of justice and peace have all been factors that have touched my own understanding of who I am and what I feel called to be and do in relation to God, and to the life he lived among us in Jesus who is Son and servant, friend and brother.

All of this has touched and influenced my own relationships to God in prayer and with the Spirit of his Son in others, as I struggled to enter into his desires, and his tender, loving and merciful compassion for us, his children—especially for those who are marginated and destitute.

My own personal experience in a position of leadership this last decade has drawn me into a new love for the Church with the desire to live Jesus' own experience as he desires to be continually incarnate in our time. For me it has meant a change of direction from the quiet regularity and guaranteed times of solitude that a more monastic form of religious life offered, to one that has placed us in a stream of experience where we have touched and have been touched by the agony of uncertitude and insecurity that renewal brought, not only within our own lives, but also with the need that confronted us to articulate that experience in an all too often not-understanding nor comprehending relationship with those whose ultimate discernment gave meaning to our lives as religious in the Church. It further challenged us and called us forth to

search out the ways in which we might be more present to those whose lives left them feeling less than persons, whose human dignity had not been acknowledged and whose own gifts needed to be called forth in an enabling sense.

My prayer these years, as a result of that experience, has taken me to the Gospel and the life of Jesus who is the revealing Word of his Father in a new and more involving way. I believe, most certainly, that Jesus meets me in my own experience and that it is *there* in relating that experience to his own that I can best meet him and through his life-giving Spirit respond to the Father in searching out his will and finding him in all things.

Of particular importance to me these last years has been the person of Mary in whom I find the ability to ponder the meaning of things I do not understand, to trust in the power of the Father, to give praise to his glory. To surrender in risk with her to the revelation of God, to go out in haste and joy to bring that saving joyous word to others, to be willing to "return home again" when that service is ended, to stand with her at the presentation, to receive a word which is a sword of sorrow, to go away a little wiser yet not fully understanding—these are both challenge and consolation. Finally, to stand with her on Calvary, with the other faithful women, in the strength of powerlessness, fully present to the anguish and ocean of suffering that she cannot prevent even as she ponders the meaning of the mystery—this, for me, in the last analysis, is the only solace in the on-going suffering of Jesus that enters our world so profoundly in the plight of the poor, the persecution of the powerless, and the seeming in-

Margaret Brennan, I.H.M. is an international leader in the movement for developing houses of prayer for active congregations.

ability to assuage the agony of over half our world, most of which I cannot touch.

In the midst of unfulfilled hopes and the desolation that such sorrow often brings, I found the meaning of my experience with the disciples on the Emmaus road who did not understand the meaning of the Scriptures—who were foolish and slow of heart to believe until Jesus himself made clear the meaning of things which I, like they, too humanly hoped in, too easily tried to bring about with the strength of my own energy and endeavors. "Was it not ordained that Christ should suffer and so enter into his glory?"

Prayer for me, then, has been an entering into my own heart and experience and finding its meaning in the experience of Jesus and of his Mother who is perfect Christian and faith-filled believer.

Prayer is also the challenge to find Jesus, to respond to him, to rejoice in his goodness, and mercy, and tender love as I meet it in the men and women who speak his revealing Word to me in the encounters of every day and in the challenging, often ambiguous signs of our times. It is also in the resonating response I find within myself when I am able in turn to speak a saving word to another.

The Breviary—particularly the morning and evening prayer—is also for me a meaningful way, especially after hearing God "speak" in the world and national news, to be in the name of the Church the voice for those especially who cannot rejoice, who know not how to praise, whose sorrow is too deep except to weep and cry out, to pray for and in them to the one God who is Father of us all.

And now—at present—when my responsibilities as leader of a congregation are at an end, I find that I can enter my own heart in peace and joy, that I can receive the love of Jesus, know his Spirit, and surrender to the Father in the knowledge that it is all right to be who I am, that he loves me as I am, and that I can "let it be."

In another way, it is to begin, happily, to realize the truth I find in myself that Gail Sheehy describes so well in Passages—that "like most men (women) who have spent their early energies in being responsive to others what is needed now is time for attending to oneself . . . time out from being the man (woman) with all the answers to become the pilgrim with questions." ●

"Authentic marriage of contemplation and social witness"

ROSEMARY RADFORD RUETHER

Prayer and social actions are often made opposites of each other. This is unfortunate because prayer is really the interiority out of which any religiously based social witness must come. Without that inner base, those who speak for justice become, to quote St. Paul, "noisy gongs and clanging cymbals" (1 Cor. 13:1). More concretely, I believe that the ability to persevere under suffering and opprobrium, to be led into a sacrificial life style, to recognize and reject paths of easy fame and fortune and, above all, to remain clearly committed to the humanity of both oppressed and oppressors while seeking to change the social structures that have made them such—all this is the measure of the depths of interiority developed by the social prophet.

In my own personal development a concern for the contemplative life originally had priority over social involvement. It was only gradually that I moved into activities such as the civil rights movement, the peace movement and the women's movement and began to locate my liturgical and contemplative sensitivities in the context of social witness. My most satisfying experiences of prayer have been when there was an authentic marriage of the two. But I doubt that I would have had an idea of how social witness could express liturgy and prayer if I had not spent some years pursuing meaningful liturgy and prayer in more traditional settings.

The monastic, contemplative tradition of the Church is very important to me. I was fortunate to be associated with a Benedictine monastery on the West coast for about six years. The baroque and even the medieval developments of monasticism had been stripped off this community, and one could sense in it the simple, bracing air of desert spirituality. Here the strong individuality of early hermitism made an easy balance with communalism, but without clericalism or hierarchicalism. Even better, monasticism here had remembered that it could be a temporary life style for many people in the Church, rather than a total life style for just a few. When the thirst for prayer and contemplation grew widespread in American society a few years ago, most

people turned to esoteric traditions from Asia. The Christian contemplative tradition generally failed to make itself available to those who wanted to develop a life of prayer and solitude as a dimension of a life lived "in the world."

One of the most important fruits of contemplative life for me is the sense of inner harmony and rhythm, the grounding of the noise and fragmentedness of life on the deep unity of calm and silence. It is this experience that I point to when I think about being "grounded in God." Some people dislike the Tillichian term for God as the "ground of our being" because they regard it as impersonal. This has always been a very meaningful term for me. This term for me points to the profound at-onement with the deep unity that binds us all together both beyond and yet the foundation for the personhood of each of us. One can sustain a life of conflict, hurt and incoherence in our everyday life only by cultivating that deep sense of unity and silence as the real foundation of our being. I also feel an affinity with the Quaker tradition in this regard. I particularly like the way my Quaker activist friends start organizing meetings and take important decisions only after spending some time cultivating that sense of gatheredness in silence. It is not accidental that Catholic radicals, coming from roots in monastic life, and Quaker radicals have found a certain affinity for each other in the Peace Movement and organizing ventures such as the Movement for a New Society (see S. Gowan, G. Lakey, W. Moyer and R. Taylor, *Moving Toward a New Society*, Philadelphia, New Society Press, 1976).

Martin Buber was a very important mentor for me in the contemplative life. His concept of I-Thou encounter

Dr. Rosemary Radford Ruether is a professor at Garrett Evangelical Theological Seminary.

still provides my basic model of divine-creaturely relationship. God discloses himself not as a tyrant or master before whom the creature cowers as an abased serf that dares not lift its eyes. This model of relationship to God drawn from oppressive political power has too long tainted our religious imagination. God is disclosed as Thou. The All, the foundation of Being, appears as Person in such a way as to affirm and bestow our own personhood, our own autonomy even. Buber taught me to recognize the Thou of God disclosed through our fellow human beings, but also through other creaturely beings which at that moment of encounter also become person for us. Our Christian spirituality has too often taught us to divorce the vertical from the horizontal, the human from the other beings we call "nature."

Through Buber I discovered a prayer life that affirmed a biblical God of all creation who can be revealed through all parts of creation as Person, and who is never revealed apart from creation. One does not find heaven by despising earth, but heaven is disclosed only in the doing of God's will on earth. The earthly itself, as the Greek Orthodox tradition teaches us, thus becomes the icon of the divine.

In the middle 1960's I became involved in the civil rights movement. I spent a summer working for the Delta Ministry in Mississippi, and ten years in Washington, D.C., teaching at a black seminary and in contact with the peace and anti-imperialist groups there. Some of the most important moments in that experience for me came when our resistance to evil social power also became a gatheredness in prayer. I can remember a Stations of the Cross that went from one government department to another in solemn witness to the atrocities being committed by these branches of the American state, culminating in the simplest but most powerful experience of the Eucharist in a small park in front of the Watergate apartment. I can remember another such moment when the dry bread of a salami sandwich and a glass of water in a paper cup became a jail Eucharist. And many more. This was the bread of heaven upon which those who hungered and thirsted after justice could travel many days. ●

"Who is your neighbor?"

HELEN M. WRIGHT

No, I cannot accept. This was my first reaction to the invitation to write about my personal prayer. I felt I had to keep something for myself; I could not share everything. But then, I asked myself, where is this God with whom you want to preserve a private relationship? The answer, contained in the following paragraphs, compelled me to say yes.

That is what prayer does to me; it tears off the layers of thick skin I try to grow

Helen M. Wright, S.N.D., who holds a Ph.D. from the University of Toronto, is director of Urban Pastoral Training at the Washington Theological Coalition.

in an effort to keep "objective" and "untouched" and "whole." Prayer leaves me transparent, exposed, vulnerable to my world and to my God. And prayer gives me an agonizing joy in this experience. It is this peculiar joy that keeps me praying. I am beginning to understand a little what John meant when he describes Jesus' prayer experience in the garden—the pain of the world's people pressing in and the angels' ministering to him.

I used to think I could pray better if I did not get so involved and distracted by people and situations. Of course, I still go apart for reflection, but I am learning that, if I am not struggling to be present among those for whom Jesus had such a predilection—the poor, the alienated, the lonely—or working on their behalf, I just cannot tune in on Jesus. More and more, his people drive me to confront Jesus in their midst, to worship him, love him, beg him to give us all our daily bread.

I used to think I would be a better teacher of theology if I "kept to my profession" and worked hard at scholarly research. Certainly I have not abandoned that pursuit, but I am discovering that I cannot theologize without prayer, the special knowledge of Jesus and his truth that comes from experiencing his presence in the midst of his suffering people.

I used to think that activity and prayer were not compatible, especially when attempted simultaneously. But I am beginning to realize a peculiar intensity of God's presence when I am most painfully wrenched out of myself by trying to respond to a human need of a neighbor.

So often, I beg Jesus not to plague me with the question, "Who is your neighbor?" I can sustain the attempt to share the pain of the lonely old person down the street or even the fears of the sick in the hospital near my home. "But, Lord," I pray, "please do not ask me to take on the world—the millions who are dying of poverty and hunger and the power structures that are causing the oppression." This experience of powerlessness drives me to search out my believing community so that together we can share the weight of the suffering and together we can beg for Jesus' strength and courage to be neighbor.●

JOSEPH GOSSMAN

"Praying because I needed to pray..."

There can be no doubt about it: again in our American society we are surrounded at this time by a renewed interest in prayer. Many of our young people are involved in this effort. Personally I am encouraged and pleased by any interest and concern aimed at deepening our knowledge and experience of prayer. I believe that prayer is at the heart of our Christian lives. Prayer energizes us and our lives. Prayer in a real sense keeps us alive.

Today countless people are involved in a personal search to develop in their own lives a deeper experience of God and of his power and presence. As I move among the people of the Raleigh diocese where I serve, I sense a real hunger among them for prayer, for God and for the things of God. And this search takes place in a social and

Most Reverend F. Joseph Gossman, D.D., J.C.D. is Bishop of Raleigh.

43

cultural climate which at times seems not only indifferent to religion but even hostile and at odds with it.

Try to obtain a copy of one of Thomas Merton's books from a public library. There is an endless wait. The list of people who are waiting to read what Merton has to say about God and prayer, about life and death, and about the struggle of being faithful to God's call in our lives never seems to end. People of all ages, especially young people, are devouring the books of people like Merton and others who promise contact with God, the experience of prayer and some familiarity with what we used to call "spiritual" things.

My own experience and growth in prayer has been, I believe, interesting. In retrospect I realize now that at some time in the past I made a transition; instead of praying because I *should* pray, I began praying because I *needed* to pray. I really believe that every effort at serious prayer must come ultimately more from need than from duty. Prayer will only become what it is meant to become when it proceeds from a deeply felt need to pray. Gradually I found myself praying because I had to pray, just as I had to breathe to live. In spite of this growth that I sense, I am also very aware of how poor and insufficient my prayer often is. I know how much growth and perfection is yet possible, yet necessary for me. I pray not because I am perfect but because I believe that by means of prayer God can bring about the transformation that is still necessary for me if I am ever to reach perfection.

It is because I am aware of my need to deepen my ties with God that for the last eight years I have gone several times each year to spend some time with the Trappist monks of Berryville, Virginia, near Winchester. I go there each time to devote myself primarily to the inner search for God as it is called by some. I live in the monastery with the monks and pretty much follow their schedule. I try to spend as much time as possible in prayer and reflection.

Since leaving Baltimore where I served for five years as vicar for the city-church (or the urban vicariate as it was called) I have noticed a difference in my times at Berryville. Before coming to Raleigh as its bishop, I went to the quiet of the monastery in search of some peace, some relief from the constant pressures and problems of urban ministry and city living. Now I find that there is less "escape" in my trips to the monastery. North Carolina poses plenty of problems for me but it is not the "pressure cooker" that my former job often seemed to be. Now I find that I am "running to" much more than "running from" on my visits to the monastery each year.

And I find my prayer is different—much more centered on the Lord and less on *myself*, *my* work and *my* special needs. I say this not with any notion that I am now without needs or problems. I seem now less distracted by outside events and by outside pressures; I am left alone with Jesus. But prayer in this new way brings its own problems, for now prayer is simply Jesus and myself—a simple combination that highlights my own poverty and my own emptiness before the Holy One!

I go three times each year to the monastery for the very simple reason that I need to. I need to take the time to discover again Jesus in my life, to find how he and I are "connected" in terms of my life, my ministry, my work. It is so easy to lose a sense of that connectedness in our hurried lives—even when we are doing the Lord's own work!

Many people in our world are hungering for Jesus, hungering for a deeper prayer-relationship with God. I am one who feels that hunger too. I must take the time that is necessary to know God better and thus to love him more. That is why I go to the monastery. That is why I intend to keep going.●

"Lord, it is good for us to be here"

THOMAS H. CLANCY

Three things have strongly influenced my own life of prayer in the past few years. First there was a passage from Bob Ochs' little book, *God Is More Present Than You Think*: "Prayer of colloquy is not nearly 'colloquial' enough. Speaking with God 'exactly as one friend speaks to another,' as Ignatius Loyola flatly states it, has yet to be really explored, partly because . . . our personal relationships themselves have become so bland that we have forgotten exactly how intimate friends do speak to one another."

I try to be myself more with the Lord now. In the past, I was probably acting a lot meeker and more resigned in my prayer than I actually was. I argue more with God now and I don't make my

Thomas H. Clancy, S.J., who has his doctorate in political science from London University, is presently provincial of the New Orleans Province of the Society of Jesus.

46

peace with him prematurely. That means more time for prayer and coming in with my problems. It also means that I have had to learn how to talk with my friends on a deeper level. It has also involved learning to listen and not getting nervous when there are long silences. I am a long way from getting it right but I feel that I am on a promising track.

I also find, and this is the second point, that I have had to learn to talk with my friends about God in order to talk with God as a friend. This was made easier by my appointment as a religious superior five years ago. Superiors are supposed to talk about God, but I felt uneasy doing so chiefly because I was afraid of being laughed at or taken for a pious type. I found myself using circumlocutions like "service," "virtue," "commitment," "duty," and "self-development" without being able to speak about service or commitment to whom. I was greatly aided in "coming out for God" by my friends who proved their love by not laughing at me.

Directed retreats also helped. The director sees you on a daily basis and all he wants to talk about is: How is it with you and God? It's like learning a new language. You have to accept the fact that you're going to do it badly at first. This experience carried over into my daily life. Of course, if one doesn't pray he has little to talk about either in or out of retreat. Now I don't feel too awkward talking about God with my friends, even those who have only a marginal interest in the subject.

My friends in the charismatic renewal have also helped me learn to bring God into my conversations more naturally. Their spontaneity and joy in the Lord has made me envious of their experience. Experience is the key concept. Karl Rahner wrote somewhere that in a world that has few institutional supports for religion the only Christians in the future will be those who have an experience of God.

I experience God, feel his presence mostly with people, seeing their zeal for God and justice and worshiping with them. In my younger days I was most turned on by Benediction. Now I feel his presence most often in the liturgies that come after a day or several days of deliberations, at weddings, ordinations, anniversary Masses. Organ music still moves me but so do guitars, and I find that I feel very close to God when lustily singing some of the new church music.

Third and last, I have come back to giving our Lady a greater place in my prayer. I love the Salve Regina and the Magnificat in English or Latin, spoken or sung. The Magnificat, our Lady's hymn of praise recorded in Luke (2:46ff.), is the theme of a great deal of my prayer. She glories in God's favor and I imitate her unabashedly. After fifty-three years of his blessings I love to reflect on his goodness and how much he loves me. I have no idea why he does after my many infidelities, but it is crystal-clear to me that he does. That makes me very happy, which is another way of saying that it makes me very blessed.

There is probably not enough reverence and hope in my prayer. After years of being a semi-Deist and a semi-Pelagian, I have become soft on presumption. But all of this is a relatively new development. I pray daily for the grace of perseverance in his love and service which in my present state means that he will show himself to me and let me feel his love and presence, and all of this on a regular and frequent basis.

This is how God and I deal with each other "exactly as one friend speaks to another." Lord, it is good for us to be here. ●

"Centrality of the Eucharist in the prayer life"

LAWRENCE CARDINAL SHEHAN

The following lines are submitted to *New Catholic World* in response to the invitation of its editor to record some thoughts based on my own experience on things helpful to personal prayer. I must say that it is with some trepidation that I set forth my personal experience in a matter such as this, lest it be thought that I presume to have something of particular importance to offer, whereas in reality whatever of value I have to say must have been said many

His Eminence Lawrence Cardinal Shehan is former Archbishop of Baltimore.

times more effectively, by others. However, in this day, does one reply to such an invitation that one has nothing to say, or that in days of retirement one cannot find the time? Let this be my excuse for writing on such a delicate subject.

My first observation is that, unless one has developed, or is on the way to developing, a sense of utter dependence on God, personal prayer is pointless and indeed, in the long run, quite impossible. Here I am not speaking merely of an intellectual acceptance of the fact of such dependence which must be present in the mind of any believer. In addition to that, I am speaking of an *attitude*, a *sense*, or perhaps more correctly a conscious *acceptance of dependence* that pervades one's whole thinking, one's whole mental and emotional life, and is in the background of every thought, every decision and action. I am speaking in particular of the confidence, the Christian hope, that springs from the consciousness of the fact that we are dependent upon a God of goodness, of mercy and forgiveness, whose highest concrete expression is our Lord and Savior Jesus Christ. It is this atmosphere of dependence, confidence and gratitude that produces growth in that love of God which is the very substance of personal prayer.

It is important to realize that there are certain internal conditions and external circumstances which, no matter what the intellectual convictions one begins with, can weaken and even destroy one's sense of confidence in God —certain health conditions, certain personal associations, social aims in which one can easily become involved, especially in these days in which the social mission of the Church is receiving so much emphasis, current concepts of self-fulfillment which are so prominent—which, if not controlled, become incompatible with the sense or attitude of complete dependence on and confidence in God.

To illustrate the effect of physical condition on one's sense of confidence in God, I believe it may be proper to take as an example the case of the great saint, Paul of the Cross. If I remember correctly, his earliest official biographer dwells at some length on the long periods of utter desolation, of a seeming loss of confidence in God, of something that almost amounted to despair, that beset him in the later period of his life. This his early biographer attributed in large measure to temptation of the devil, to which God allowed him to be subjected in order to bring him in the end to a total abandonment of self and a more complete union with God. I am not questioning the reality of such external causes. But to understand such experiences in such a person, it seems to me that one ought to begin by considering natural causes that are capable of bringing them about and only then turn to the praeternatural and supernatural. The plain fact is that Paul had by nature a body that was delicate and sensitive. For many years he had subjected it to long, hard fasts, to frequent vigils, to intense mortifications; and he had driven it unmercifully to hard work, to long journeys on foot through all kinds of weather, over all sorts of terrain. Add to this the sense of great frustration that he experienced, when he found his spiritual and religious goals successfully blocked, to all appearances, by forces almost completely unanticipated. It was, then, quite natural that he would be the subject of prolonged periods of depression, of self-questioning, even of seeming doubt.

Perhaps I am inclined to exaggerate the importance of such causes and to underestimate the spiritual and supernatural forces by which one might expect them to be overcome by an experience of my own life. Here let me say I do not presume to compare my own trivial experience with that of the saint. I simply undertake to illustrate how natural and physical conditions and external causes can sometimes react on the individual's mental and emotional life and seriously impair one's ability to engage in personal prayer. Toward the end of my rather long seminary training (twelve years from entrance into the preparatory or minor seminary to completion of the courses of philosophy and theology in the major seminary), while I was a student in the North American College in Rome, I experienced a somewhat prolonged period of mental depression, of frustration, of a sense of hopelessness in the face of a future that seemed dark and hopeless. The causes were not far to seek, in the eyes of an outside observer, sensitive, experienced and wise.

When the rector learned of my mental state and my growing conviction that I ought to quit and perhaps give up entirely the intention of pursuing the priesthood, he directed me to see the house physician who was an excellent diagnostician and a man of wide experience, not always fully appreciated by students. As a result of a physical examination, the doctor sent me off to a *casa di cura,* overlooking beautiful Lake Nemi, where I underwent a minor operation and spent several weeks recuperating with nourishing food supplied by the sisters who conducted the *casa.* That, followed by several weeks with some fellow students at Andermat in Switzerland, quickly changed both my health and my mental outlook. The following autumn I was able to resume and complete my studies with fair success, and to receive priestly ordination in due time. This I present not as a world-shaking experience but as a practical example of how bodily health and external circumstances can affect one's spiritual life and interfere with one's ability to engage in fruitful personal prayer. As I later looked back on the experience, I came to the conclusion that my difficulties arose mainly from two causes: the insufficient diet, which in the Italy of post-World War I

seemed alone to be available to seminaries and other institutions forced to operate on a very restricted budget, and an overly ambitious program of studies without the physical resources to sustain such a program. The ancient proverbs are always valid: "mens sana in corpore sano" and "ne quid nimis" (nothing in excess).

Just as it is important to realize that certain bodily and psychological conditions and external circumstances can seriously impede the practice of personal prayer, so, too, it is important to realize that other such internal conditions and external circumstances can safeguard and promote prayer. Actually, such adverse conditions patiently borne and successfully overcome can be the occasion of spiritual profit and advancement in personal prayer. It may even be that my own painful experience was the occasion of ultimate spiritual profit.

A recent book by Herbert Benson, M.D., associate professor in the Harvard Medical School, entitled *The Relaxation Response* (William Morrow & Co., N.Y., 1975), deals at some length with the interrelation between certain physical and emotional conditions and what he calls the meditative technique. Quite naturally, as a physician, he is primarily interested in the effect of prayer on bodily and mental welfare. In the section on the basic elements of meditation he quotes at some length some Catholic mystics, notably St. Augustine, St. Teresa of Avila, and certain medieval mystics. Dr. Benson points out that meditation and personal prayer are in harmony with our natural mechanisms which serve to counterbalance stress and tensions through relaxation response. Thus personal prayer contributes to our natural health and sense of well-being.

Of all the saints whose lives are familiar to me, none so well illustrates the importance of a constant sense of utter dependence on God, the sense of confidence that arises from the total acceptance of such dependence on the goodness and mercy of our Lord and Savior, and the gratitude to, and love of, God that are fostered by such dependence and confidence, as that of St. Francis of Assisi. Recently in preparing a talk for the 750th anniversary of the death of Francis, I had occasion to turn back to the *Life of St. Francis of Assisi*, by the Danish convert, Johannes Jörgensen, written at the beginning of this century and available now in the reasonably priced paperback Image books. It is, I believe, still the best life of St. Francis we have, although the value of Father Cuthbert's *Life* and Chesterton's rather long essay is not to be underestimated. Those concerned with their advancement in personal prayer would do well to possess and read Jörgensen's *Life*.

I fear that I have already exceeded the thousand-word limit placed on these observations. There are just two things that I would add: the importance of fixing a definite time each day for the practice of personal prayer, and the necessity for a Catholic to make Christ in the Eucharist the center of such prayer. From my own experience, I would say that unless our schedule of life provides for the regular practice of personal prayer, there is the danger that it will cease to be a major or even a real force in life. There is the likelihood that we shall find ourselves substituting other things for it, particularly what we consider useful work, or urgent business, or community interest.

As for the centrality of the Eucharist in the prayer life of any Catholic, this should be so obvious as to need no fur-

ther development. As a priest, the daily offering of the sacrifice of the Mass is so important to me that, were I to be deprived of the privilege, I can well imagine my prayer life, such as it is, soon falling to pieces. This I believe is true of most priests. Nor is it less true of the Catholic layman that the Eucharist must, almost of necessity, be the center of prayer for him.

Certainly this seems to be true of the small but prayerful group of the laity who daily attend the Mass I offer at the old Cathedral Church in downtown Baltimore. The group is fairly well divided between young and old, men and women. I am particularly impressed with two rather young men who rarely are absent—particularly with the younger. Apparently he is in his early or middle twenties, a very normal looking individual with nothing odd or pretentious in his general conduct or his devotion. Each morning when I arrive in church to prepare for Mass, he is already kneeling before the altar of the Blessed Sacrament, absorbed in prayer. Each morning he receives Communion with great reverence and simplicity and then shortly he is gone, I suppose to his daily work.

The other is a man apparently somewhat older. Each day he appears in what I take are neat laborer's clothes. He is equally devout and equally simple and unpretentious in his devotion. Strange to say, I have never had the occasion to converse at any length with either of them. I do not know their names or where they live. They seem to be there simply because they find Christ there in the Eucharist. For them, the Eucharist obviously is the very center of their prayer life. For anyone, priest or lay person, who practices personal prayer, that is quite as it should be.●

"Since we live by the Spirit, let us follow the Spirit's lead"

JOHN J. DOUGHERTY

The thoughts I shall set down here will be concerned with prayer as reflection or meditation. They are the fruit of the effort and experience of forty years. I prefer the word reflection, or reflective prayer, as more descriptive of this kind of prayer, since the initial act, it seems to me, is a turning inward.

Most Reverend John J. Dougherty, S.T.L., S.S.D. is Auxiliary Bishop of Newark.

Reflective prayer has to do with consciousness, ongoing inner awareness or perception. Conscious life comprises the totality of our impressions, thoughts and feelings. The engagement of consciousness is related to our bodiness and our ambience. In winter I am conscious of chill; at a concert I am conscious of music. Consciousness is ordinarily and routinely occupied with the stimuli coming from the mind, the body, the emotions, the senses, and from the external experiences of our days and hours.

Reflective prayer is a turning inward, a withdrawal to some degree from all of this. It is not answering the door to the knocking. When the knocking stops, and the quiet comes, consciousness can begin to direct itself, to take over the controls. First, it directs itself to an awareness of power that comes from believing, to the recognition and the conviction that "we do not know how to pray as we ought; but the Spirit himself makes intercession for us with groanings that cannot be expressed in speech" (Rom. 8:26), that "since we live by the Spirit, let us follow the Spirit's lead" (Gal. 5:25).

In view of this it seems appropriate to begin with the plea, "Let the silence come upon me which is the silence of God. Let the power be released in me which is the Spirit of God."

One may ask what direction the controlled consciousness should primarily take. Inward or upward? Horizontal or vertical? Terrestrial or transcendental. The question does not seem to me to be of first importance. The transcendent God is also immanent. The creator is present to his creation. God is within us as well as "up there." I believe that all the indicated directions are part of reflective prayer, and that we should "follow the Spirit's lead." Since we share the Spirit that was in Jesus, we may expect that the Spirit will lead our consciousness to Jesus, and that his words will resound and fill the silence of God.

It was in the same Spirit that Jesus saw his heavenly Father feeding birds of the air. The terrestrial was transparent to the heavenly. The recorded words of Jesus should echo through the chambers of the inner silence. A man reveals himself in his speech, and the Son of Man revealed himself and his Father in his words. His words were also a revelation of ourselves and our needs. In the inner silence we should look at the behavior of Jesus, what he did and how he did it. His presence was a healing presence, his touch was a healing touch, his words were a healing sound. The Gospels are our most authentic portrait of Jesus, the portrait we must contemplate with longing. In this contemplative prayer we experience his healing presence and begin to absorb his kind of love, and the fire of that love makes our selfish love wither and our altruistic love grow.

The Spirit we have received is a life-giving Spirit. There is no life without breath and prayer is the breath of the soul. Not to pray is to languish spiritually and to die. Breathing is a personal activity. No one else can do it for me. In like manner no one else can do my reflective prayer for me. It is personal, it is individual, it is unique. There are other kinds of prayer, but without this breathing I may be lifeless to them and they to me.

Secondly, there is shared prayer, a group sharing its reflections. We priests meet weekly with the sisters in the convent for shared prayer. I consider it meaningful, helpful, supportive. I believe it will be that as long as the participants have prayed well in solitude. The benefit, as I see it, rests in the sharing of the collective consciousness. A reflective response to a Scripture reading is rarely, if ever, identical in two listeners. The response is conditioned by the consciousness of the individual listener, which is the existen-

54

tial totality of impressions, thoughts and feelings of the individual person. The listeners bring to the hearing of the Word varying degrees of knowledge, openness, sensitivities, experience, unselfishness and agapic love. But an honest sharing of the collective consciousness can help build Christian community, and Christian community can help build Christians, and, like all people, Christians need one another.

In the Catholic tradition there exists a rich treasure of recorded collective consciousness, the shared prayer of the Fathers of the Church, the doctors and the saints. Think, for example, of the words of Ignatius of Antioch, the prayers and hymns of Francis of Assisi, the writings of Teresa of Avila and Thérèse of Lisieux, and Elizabeth Ann Seton. Their words and thoughts make worthy entry into the silence of God, and by sharing them we may breathe in the life-giving Spirit.

Upon these stones of personal and shared prayer liturgical prayer will firmly and stoutly rest. The Liturgy of the Hours is in my judgment a most noteworthy book of prayer. If reflective prayer is essential to savoring its beauty, the breviary can in turn serve as gracious food for the soul's nourishment and delight. The liturgy of the Eucharist is worship as well as memorial. The memorial of Jesus' death is made visible in the sacramental sign of bread and wine, and the worship is made visible in the worshiping demeanor of the celebrant and the people. Without reflective prayer that worshiping sign will not be made visible. Wedded inseparably to personal prayer it will rise as a standard proclaiming to the people that Jesus Christ is Lord. ●

"The sounds of silence"

BERARD L. MARTHALER

We understand it when we speak of it; we understand also when we hear it spoken of by another. What then is prayer? If no one asks me, I know; if I wish to explain it, I know not. This paraphrase of St. Augustine describes my experience and, I suspect, it is an

Berard L. Marthaler, O.F.M. Conv., S.T.D., Ph.D. is chairman of the department of religion and religious education at Catholic University of America.

experience shared by the majority of religious people in all traditions. To paraphrase again (this time Stephen Leacock, I think) those who can, pray; those who can't, talk about it.

If I were to attempt to teach another how to pray I would follow two courses. First, I would do what my mother (and later my novice master) did, namely, schedule certain moments for prayer, however brief, create an atmosphere conducive to prayer, and pray with me from time to time. One learns to pray by praying. And second, I would tell stories—parables and allegories—illustrating the efficacy of prayer.

But my purpose here is not to teach. It is to share some random impressions based largely on my own experiences and observations.

It is important to disabuse ourselves of the idea that prayer is a dialogue. A dialogue suggests a colloquy, a reasoned exchange of ideas and information. To think of prayer in these terms leads ultimately, if not inevitably, to frustration because prayer is not a matter of give and take. Prayer may be a response to a revealed message or an address to the One who has called us, but it is not a dialogue. Prayer is more important for the attitude that it expresses than for the information it communicates.

If it is not the nature of prayer to communicate, it is to "commune." Whereas dialogue conjures up a conversation that is public and formal, communion suggests intercourse that is private and discursive. Dialogue cannot be carried on without words. The language of communion is often silence. Intimacy—union with—is the object of prayer. It strengthens trust and acknowledges need. Prayer expresses dependency, a dependence which enables because one basks in the goodness and greatness of life and love at its Source.

The root problem, however, is not how one describes prayer. One's inability to pray stems from a loss of all sense of divine presence. The great mystics acknowledged periods in which it was all but impossible to pray because they felt abandoned and alone. In the marrow of their being they experienced only the cold and dark of starless nights. The eclipse of God is the source of much malaise in our time. While the slogan "God is dead" has lost its edge, the poignancy of void and meaninglessness is suffered by many.

One of the works that made a great impression on me in my formative years was Abbé Chautard's *The Soul of the Apostolate*. Like other works of that kind it suggested aids to "practicing the presence of God." A pause from the hectic pace of the daily grind, a moment of silence to regain one's serenity, ejaculations uttered under one's breath—these are such obvious techniques that they hardly need mentioning, but they do need cultivating. While my world is no longer that of Chautard, Abbot Marmion and Edward Leen, I find that some of the behavior patterns of long ago are still with me.

"Practicing the presence of God" needs to be worked at (though I am not so Pelagian as to suggest that the initiative is mine). It is a matter of learning to interpret signs, of not allowing the obvious to distract us from deeper reality. Practicing the presence of God is more than affirming his omnipresence as philosophers do. It means bringing this presence to consciousness, of raising it to a level where God's proximity can be felt. The divine presence seems more real in those ecstatic moments—"peak experiences" —when we are taken out of ourselves, but ecstasy is a rarity. The challenge is to make the presence of God an experiential reality in both the humdrum routine and hectic activity of everyday living. I find my capacity for prayer is measured in proportion to my awareness of the divine presence.

There are many paradoxical aspects to prayer. Several are linked to language. One cannot pray without words, yet words distract. They seem banal before the grandeur who is God, mere chatter in the presence of Truth. One finds that he falls back on some of the prayer formulas he has learned in his youth: the Angelus, St. Francis' prayer for peace, and ejaculatory formulas. They are preferable to the inane sentimentalities and pretentious or platitudinous prose of much of what passes for "spontaneous prayer."

Better than all words are "the sounds of silence." The sounds of silence form the kind of speech my parents use after more than fifty years together. Even when they are not talking, they are communing; when they speak to one another their words convey meaning that eludes the ears of a bystander, even though he or she has been close to them for almost all those years. The sounds of silence are the quiet decibels of profound speech that vibrate through one's being; they are the lyrics of communion, the music of mystery. Silence is not merely the absence of noise, a deafening void. Silence sharpens one's hearing, hones one's reflexes, and makes one sensitive to movement, however slight, even before it can be seen. In silence one comes to grips with his or her own identity and is overcome by his or her dependence on the Other. In these moments words are incidental to prayer because everything worth saying and doing has already been said and done.●

FRANCIS S. MacNUTT

"Prayer for healing"

In the past eight years my own prayer has been radically transformed—but not in the way I would have expected.

For years my life of prayer, like that of many friends, was a constant search for time and solitude. Then, after finding the time and solitude, I experienced an occasional deep touch of the presence of God, much peace (if I could pray long enough), and, still more often, aridity. At these times of dryness I would pace slowly up and down the

Francis S. MacNutt, O.P. holds a Ph.D. in theology and is a leading charismatic preacher.

chapel, and this would bring a kind of healing peace by its very rhythm.

What I would have expected to see if my prayer improved was (a) a more determined decision to seek time and solitude (b) followed hopefully by more of the gift of prayer, evidenced in a deeper awareness of God.

I still believe in that, but now I know a different dimension of prayer that I didn't even expect. It's a dimension of the prayer of petition—that lowly, first form of prayer that I think is underestimated. For I now find that about

59

three-quarters of my time of prayer, sometimes up to eight hours a day, is *for* and *with* other people.

The turning point was a workshop on prayer for healing that I made in 1968 with Mrs. Agnes Sanford and Rev. Tommy Tyson as its teachers. This opened up a whole new world. Before this time I conceived of prayer almost exclusively in terms of getting away from the confusion of life to pray, either alone or in common. I knew that there was an ideal of praying always, that our work, too, in some way is a prayer, that our minds can become more constantly aware of God, as the atmosphere of life, much as a person in love thinks constantly of the beloved. But somehow the confusion of life always seemed like a distraction, compared to the pure water of the prayer of solitude.

What I have learned is that the pain, the confusion of life is the very substance of prayer with other people. At one time I thought of the prayer of Jesus in terms of his times of solitude when he fled from the crowds—and even ran away from his disciples long before dawn—in order to be with his Father on the mountaintops.

Somehow it never struck me that most of his prayer was with the people; it was prayer for healing—and he spent hours at it. In fact, a main thrust of his work as Savior was healing the sick and casting out demons, bringing in the Kingdom of God and routing the kingdom of darkness.

At one time I never conceived of my prayer life as up to imitating Jesus in that; it has been only in the past eight years that I have found I can confidently pray with people for the sicknesses

and various problems that beset them. And they are healed or helped in extraordinary ways. In the beginning I was hesitant to reach out my hand to touch a person and pray for God's help because I felt it presumptuous to expect anything to happen. It was too much like pretending I was holy or a saint. But after the teachers of the workshop convinced me that the New Testament assumed that any Christian had the privilege of asking in order to receive, I developed a little more courage and began in small ways to pray for the sick.

Since then all kinds of marvelous things have happened; we have seen cancer cured, twisted bones straightened, severe scoliosis (s-shaped curvature of the spine) straightened out, an optic nerve regenerated, glaucoma cured, deafness healed and many other ailments disappear. Truly, we have seen the deaf hear, the blind see again and the lame walk.

Far more important, of course, than all the healing of physical ailments are the inner spiritual and emotional healings that take place when we pray for people who suffer from depression, from alcoholism, from various forms of sexual compulsion and, above all, from bitterness and resentment.

I say "we" because ordinarily I work with a team praying for people for the various sufferings that oppress them. I am beginning to see more clearly why Jesus had to get away to the mountain solitude. It's because compassionate prayer works; many of the sick walk away rejoicing because they have been healed. And their friends hear and appear at our doorstep.

Not that everyone is healed; I would estimate that about twenty-five percent of those we pray for are healed completely; another fifty percent are improved in varying degrees, and for another twenty-five percent nothing external seems to happen. But (like Lourdes) everyone receives some kind of interior blessing, a sense of how much God cares, of how much he loves them.

My rediscovery of the power of the prayer of petition means that now when I am out giving a talk or a retreat, the better part is when we pray for people afterward. Sometimes this goes on for hours with lines of people, or occasionally we pray privately for as long as eight hours with one person. While I am praying with the person (often in tongues) I am concentrating on God (as best I can) and on the person. No longer is this work a distrac-tion, then, but it's as if prayer itself has become the apostolate.

Sometimes you can even feel the power of God move through the person asking for prayer. Just as Luke de-scribes power going out from Jesus, even when he wasn't saying a prayer in words, so we find that this power of healing prayer is more than words.

I see healing prayer as being an aware-ness of the love of Jesus in me that I can share with others—sometimes by word, sometimes by touch. And his love in them, in turn, returns to me in the form of thanks and lifts on up to the Father in praise.

The discovery is this: you can know the risen Christ in you; and if you will let him, he will heal the sick.●

"Lord, I believe; help my unbelief"

ELIZABETH CARROLL

For me personal prayer is the interior dialogue with God which accompanies and orders and enspirits my life. Personal prayer depends totally on faith.

I had prayed as a child, dutifully, to a God out there in the beyond of the skies and to Jesus in the tabernacle beside the flickering light and even within my heart for the few moments after Holy Communion. That devotionalism ended in struggle, the struggle to believe. Is God? Does God reveal, relate? Is Christ God? Does the Church enflesh Christ?

Out of that struggle came a will to believe. The pain of the struggle led me to value faith and to make of the prayer "Lord, I believe; help my unbelief" a basic expression of need. I find faith a fragile gift, often assaulted within our Church, in our society; a gift to be ever anew shored up by the will to believe, the prayer for faith.

Having made the original leap of faith, I was willing to surrender to that God whom I conceived as holding all the trumps. Since then God has grown for me as reality, as mystery and as life. Dialogue with that reality offered meaning and self-valuing; intimacy with that life gave me strength and courage and love; awareness of the mystery made me humble and searching. With God developed the glorious, rocky, searching, peaceful, formative, painful relationship which I call prayer. It is my ongoing reflection upon and struggle with the events of my world in the presence of a personal God who is Truth and Love and Spirit.

In this reflection the Bible, especially the New Testament, has been formative. God as creator, as relating, as faithful has come to form for me the constant horizon of my thoughts. Throughout my life I have had an intuitive need, in order to be at peace with myself, to do what is right. Prayer has been the testing of that "right" against the horizon of God's judgments.

The great discovery of my life has been the love that Jesus teaches, the love that Jesus is. A whole reordering of

Elizabeth Carroll, R.S.M., who has her Ph.D. in history from Catholic University of America, is presently a staff associate of the Center of Concern.

prayer has centered about my desire to become a loving person. The demands which Jesus makes upon me in terms of neighbor (all persons in the world as well as my closest associates, including my enemies) put me in a continuously petitionary posture. Only the realization of Christ's presence within me ever promoting love gives my prayer hope.

Another change in my prayer in the last decade has been my greater consciousness of the Spirit as a dynamic within myself but even more as a dynamic within the stance of the Church and the movement of secular society. Prayer thus becomes much more of a plea for enlightenment: to find the Lord's design in Scripture, to interpret the past and the present so as to discern the values to be embraced in the future.

As a woman in the Church I find that I need prayer as a refuge when my sense of personhood is battered by rejection and exclusion. I need prayer as a support to love when I am shaken by anger at the arrogance of structures and persons. I need prayer as forgiveness when in my turn I tend to be arrogant. I need prayer as union with my God when I sense the fragility of my being in the immense expanse of time and space. I need prayer to say thank you for all the many people who lead me to and model for me the various aspects of God. I need prayer in order to approach death with equanimity. ●

"Meditating on the Word's meaning"

MARY COLLINS

More than a decade ago the matter was first put to me: "Tell me about your mystical experiences." The occasion was a dinner party. The inquirer was the husband of a college classmate, a man I was meeting for the first time.

The bluntness of the question surprised me, although it was not without context. He was a researcher at the Na-

Mary Collins, O.S.B., Ph.D. is currently president of The Liturgical Conference and professor at the University of Kansas.

tional Institute of Mental Health, working on the effects of hallucinogenic drugs on mental states. Religiously, he was an agnostic. I was a graduate student in religion and a professed Benedictine sister garbed in traditional religious habit. I had asked him what he thought of claims that drug-induced states of altered consciousness were comparable to the experiences of religious mystics. He said, as scientists will, that no data were available for comparison. Then came the request: "Tell me about your mystical experiences."

What I answered, I don't now recall. But I have never forgotten the chagrin of the moment, the embarrassment of discovering that I might be liable to charges of violating truth-in-packaging norms. Yes, I was a professed religious. Still, the expectation that I was thereby a mystic seemed unfair. Nevertheless, the matter has been there to be dealt with openly for more than a decade now. What is the quality of my prayer? What is its inspiration?

Put simply, I continue to pray in very traditional ways, ways which have been handed on to me as part of the Benedictine monastic heritage within the Catholic Church. I have continually tried to probe that heritage more deeply and to exploit its resources more fully. Because I continue to be nurtured by it and have not in any way exhausted its power for my Christian life, I have not ventured far from it.

I read Scripture with the Church daily in preparation for or in response to the daily liturgical celebrations. I meditate upon its meaning for my life in our world today. I try to open myself to the Spirit praying within me.

In reading Scripture with the Church daily, the texts abound: lessons from the hours, lessons from the Eucharist, psalms and canticles, antiphons and acclamations. From the abundance of each day's and each season's offerings I select what I will meditate. I try to be orderly—but not rigorously so. At times I have selected a single psalm for a day or a week. At other times I reflect upon the series of continuous readings from the Gospels or the prophets or the historical narratives. Occasionally I attend to the brief sentences the Church holds up as antiphons or acclamations during a liturgical season.

How much do I read and for how long? An elderly prayerful monk told me his method almost twenty years ago: read as much as you want to, as long as you care to. I have never really improved on that formula, although I understand it better now. When I am preoccupied and distracted, I tend to read longer, to reread a passage several times in its larger context, until the Word begins to engage me. When I am more tranquil, the Word engages me more quickly and I tend to read less.

In meditating on the Word's meaning for my life in our world today, several different approaches commonly help me to mull the Word over in order to take it in and be nourished by it. I repeat the text slowly, phrase by phrase, savoring the words in order to discover their power, their paradox, or their challenge. Not infrequently, the day's activities continue to resound even after I have begun to meditate on a text. When this happens, whether there is evident bearing or not, I allow the insistent concerns to sound as a counterpoint to my listening to Scripture. As a result of this dual engagement by competing voices, my meditation may be a contending with the Word rather than a simple attending to it. I disagree, argue, object, propose alternatives, all the while grateful that the psalms themselves, the Book of Job, and the example of many of our forebears in the faith have taught me that contending with God may be a part of readiness for prayer.

Not all days and seasons are times of contending. More ordinarily, I may probe the biblical passage further, either through Jerusalem Bible marginal notes and footnotes which lead me to associations and parallels or through the Jerome Biblical Commentary, where a scholar's note may guide me.

Sporadically, I write out parts of my dialogue with the Word in a small notebook. On rare occasions, I have tried to embody my meditation or readiness for prayer in movement, posture, or gesture. More often, it is an inner conversation.

In opening myself to the Spirit praying within me, the activity of meditation finally must yield to quiet, to silence, to waiting. At times the prayer which comes is one of reluctant surrender in the spirit of Jeremiah: "You duped me, Lord, and I let myself be duped." At times it is a prayer of wonder in the spirit of Paul: "How deep are the riches and the wisdom and the knowledge of God! How inscrutable his judgments, how unsearchable his ways!" It may be the prayer of the outcast blind beggar and the Canaanite woman: "Lord, have pity on me," the inspiration for the Jesus prayer of Orthodox Christianity. The prayer may be a word of confidence in the spirit of the psalmist, "I place all my trust in you, my God; all my hope is in your mercy." The prayer may be an extended wordless moment of quiet communion, broken finally by the call to turn to the more mundane tasks of my life.

This pattern of biblical-liturgical prayer continues to confirm my belief that the Word of God is living and active. It has not only deepened my capacity to hear the ritual proclamation of the Word in the Church's public worship. It has sharpened my receptivity to the challenge of the Gospel. It has made me aware of the resourcefulness I have and the limits of my resources. It has made me conscious of what we might hope to become together as Church by God's kindness and mercy, namely, the redeemed and healing community.

This quite traditional form of Christian prayer demands regularity—an established time, a familiar place. Those supports are difficult for me to maintain in these middle years of my life. Currently, I travel fairly extensively—short distances, from the university to the motherhouse for a weekend; longer distances, for an overnight stay on business. My room is somebody else's guest room. My schedule becomes erratic, my opportunities for patterned solitude interfered with by commitments to others, both early morning and late evening. My energy runs low.

I make what adjustments I can. Sometimes I am reduced to carrying a pocket New Testament and a single sheet commentary from a homily service in my overnight case. I might wish for the more ordered and tranquil world of my own past. That may yet come again in another phase of my life. Meanwhile, this pattern of prayer handed down from past generations keeps me in touch with my past even while it sustains and extends my confidence that our present and our future are ultimately in God's hands. ●

GERARD
AUSTIN

"God's love for us"

I suppose the first thing I should say about my own prayer-life is that I desperately need to pray. I have found that out the hard way. Of this I am certain: I must have prayer in my life—both communal prayer and private prayer—and the focus for both must be the Mass.

My biggest problem is the common one, of being too busy. From my own experience and from the experience of others, I know this is a crucial issue. Life is so cluttered, so noisy. I must learn to slow down, to be more still. I must let my daily encounters in silence with God spill over more into my ordinary day. This does not necessarily mean that I must do less during the

day, but it does mean that I need to program my life more faithfully, to leave time for space, space to "listen" more attentively. While clock-watching can be a dangerous illusion, nevertheless there is a certain minimum time that we should spend in personal prayer each day. Indeed, there is something very sacred, very healing, in putting this time aside and being faithful to it. In the long run, the only true test is our faithfulness, our perseverance in prayer.

While I believe this firmly, I know it can be misunderstood. I can think that

Gerard Austin, O.P. is director of the Liturgical Studies Program at Catholic University of America.

I am saving myself by my own efforts. Nothing can be further from the truth and nothing can be more destructive to a life of prayer. I think we must be convinced that God is "running the show," otherwise we shall never be ready or able to pray.

Let me put it another way. A necessary prerequisite for prayer is a living conviction that we are loved by God. For me it is put most succinctly and most beautifully in 1 John 4: "This is the love I mean: not our love for God, but God's love for us when he sent his Son to be the sacrifice that takes our sins away."

To the extent that I have forgotten that, my life of prayer has suffered. God loves me. Of that I can be perfectly certain. When I doubt it, I glance at a crucifix, for Jesus crucified is the proof that I am loved. To the extent that I grasp that (and it fluctuates greatly in my life), my prayer becomes more "passive." To the extent that I grasp it, I feel convinced that God will let me know what he wants of me. This frequently takes the form of "letting go." In this respect I often think of the call of Abraham in Chapter 12 of Genesis: "Leave your country, your family, and your father's house, for the land I will show you." It is not the land of my own choice, but where God wishes to lead me. To discern this, I must be still, I must let myself be loved, I must put the focus on God rather than on myself.

To the extent that I violate this, I turn in on myself, and my prayer becomes something akin to narcissism. Vision narrows and a thousand-and-one duties and obligations become the focus of attention, even during prayer time. This "spell" is broken in various

ways. Often God uses another human person in the process. The beauty of God's grace shines forth in the life of someone and calls me out of myself to the giver of all good things. At other times it is the awareness (or the experience) of my own sinfulness. This brings home immediately to me the utter gratuitousness of God's love. I cannot do it of myself. God is "running the show" in my life, and this is at one and the same time my consolation and my challenge.

Experience has shown me that I must have prayer in my life—both communal prayer and private prayer—and the focus for both must be the Mass. This "centering" in and through the Mass has become increasingly important for my prayer in recent years. All that I am and do becomes explicit when I bring it to the Eucharist.

The Christian life is a journey, to the Father, through the Son, in the Holy Spirit. When we offer the Eucharist the victim is not just the God-Man Christ, it is the whole Christ, head and members. St. Augustine said to his people one day at Mass: "It is the mystery of you yourselves that is on the altar; you are in the bread, you are in the cup" (Sermon 229). I myself am on that altar with Christ, offering my life and all that that contains as spiritual sacrifices acceptable to God through Jesus Christ (1 Peter 2:5). The *Constitution on the Church* of Vatican II phrased it: "During the celebration of the Eucharist, these sacrifices are most lovingly offered to the Father along with the Lord's body" (n. 34).

Thus I see (or try to see) my prayer life more and more as one reality. It is something that makes me one—one with Christ and one with all his members. Anything that in any way hinders that unity must be purged from my life. That is why my prayer often consists of asking for healing, most often for healing "in general," since God knows better than I where the work needs to be done.

It is an enormous task—to be one with Christ and all his members, and one which will never be completed in this life. So, day after day, I ask the grace to continue. I ask the grace to sing to the Lord each day "a new song"—that one day all may be completed: that I may be totally healed, that I may be totally one with Jesus Christ and all his members in a unity that, in the Holy Spirit, leads to our common Father.●

Writing about prayer is both intriguing and frustrating. If my own personal experience of prayer can be helpful to anyone else, it is worth the effort of putting it into words. But describing prayer is like describing breathing or eating. The mechanics can be put onto paper but the experience—its joy, power, meaning, attraction—is richer than human language. In fact, what sounds simple and forthright to some sounds banal and naive to others. Yet it is good for all of us to know that others pray, for in God's family we all depend on the prayers of one another.

As a theologian, my life is rather unique. Everything revolves around God: my research, writing, teaching, ministry. Whatever causes distractions in prayer for others tends to lead me deeper into prayer. Either I share in God's love and concern for some person or project or idea or social problem, or I have some sinful attitude or attachment like pride, anger, or indifference. Either circumstance easily leads me into prayer.

In a sense I have no choice about praying. God fills my mind and heart. When my mind is idling along, it drifts back to him—for example, when I am walking through Golden Gate Park or driving on a freeway or heading for class through the corridors of the university. Sometimes I talk to him aloud, which does evoke some curious glances from passers-by. But listening to God and sharing his presence is much more consoling than listening to the news or worrying about the next task facing me. One of the best things that happened to me recently was the discovery that I have diabetes. I have had to work much more exercise into my life so as to keep down the level of blood sugar. And the time spent jogging or

"Whoever sings, prays twice"

FRANCIS J. BUCKLEY

Francis J. Buckley, S.J. is professor of dogmatic theology and catechetics at the University of San Francisco and a former president of the College Theology Society.

doing calisthenics has meant more time for prayer. Jogging is quite boring, which is why so many joggers look miserable. But if it is an opportunity to be with a loved one, it can be a joy.

I enjoy prayer. Whenever I advert to God's presence, I smile, at least inwardly. Even when nothing "happens" at prayer, when there is no particular problem to discuss or mystery to ponder, I enjoy just being with God, alone. For friends and lovers talk is not needed, only presence.

Besides my teaching I work on a team of authors. This is often exhausting, especially under the pressure of deadlines. Tempers get frayed. The mind goes blank. We violently disagree on the approach to an issue. When this happens, we sit there and pray. Prayer breaks through the logjams, helps us see things in perspective, a different perspective than our own. Alas, one of the most humiliating effects of prayer is that after it I am almost always the one who has to give in to the rest of the team. But I would much rather be open to God's ideas than be limited to my own.

There are times when I am too tired for normal prayer, even too tired to just sit in the chapel or my room and be with God. At those moments I sing hymns. Hymns move me on a deep, non-rational level. Several hymnals have divided the contents according to seasons of the year or topical themes: sorrow, joy, thanksgiving, unity. Augustine wrote, "Whoever sings, prays twice," but sometimes it is the only way to pray.

The high points of my prayer come during the liturgy of the Eucharist and penance, when I am the celebrant or a concelebrant. I have learned by experience the wisdom of the Second Vatican Council's insistence on active participation in the liturgy. Praying the eucharistic prayers aloud, concentrating on their meaning for this particular congregation, trying to bring this out by phrasing, emphasis, and tone is deeply challenging and satisfying. These are moments of intense awareness of God.

Ever since my ordination I have tried to give a homily at each Mass I celebrate, even if there is only one other person present. Before the new lectionary was adopted, a few Gospel passages, like the ten wise and foolish virgins, recurred very frequently during the year. Yet each time it was possible to find something new—a word, a phrase, a nuance, an application—for I had changed and the people listening had changed and God had something new to say to us that day. The new lectionary of course expands the opportunities for discovery since most of the Bible is covered during the two-year cycle. But the most remarkable aspect of this is that in the homilies I am preaching to myself as much as to the others. I am constantly amazed at how God speaks directly to my situation each day, whether I am elated or depressed, giving me a word of warning and challenge or encouragement and support.

Something similar happens in confession. As I am talking over Scripture with a penitent or we are praying together, it is astonishing how God lets me see the sinfulness in myself and my need to follow the very advice I give. Father Michael Scanlan, T.O.R., author of *The Power in Penance*, persuaded me to pray with the penitents for wisdom to know what one step God was asking of them, and for the power to take that step with his help. The effects of that prayer are truly remarkable. We both become aware of the presence of the Holy Spirit. Sometimes the penitent will weep. Sometimes I will. As a result, I try to do all I can to make my fellow priests and penitents conscious of the prayer-possibilities of penance. In the past we have focused on ourselves rather than on God in this sacrament and so we have limited the results we expected from it. Once we rediscover that it is a prayer, enormous power is unleashed. That all who read this article may experience for themselves the prayerful nature and power of penance—and indeed of all of Christian life—is my prayer.●

"Abba, Father!"

JOSEPH TETLOW

This is about prayer, so it must begin where prayer begins: with God, who is Father, Son, and Spirit.

Who God is, we cannot say. That he is, I think we know, pulling us out of ourselves into the world where he is the other dimensions of the world's building-blocks that otherwise would have really been nothing but a facade. But he is the other dimensions, the others more real than the facade, since blocks are more than faces.

Why he shows us this is plain: he is the truth, not in the mind, but in things, all things, and in all humankind. Paul says it (think of the Ephesians): that we have this knowledge even though we are insignificant in the world, and even though no one could explain how we know it, filled with astonishment whether we be serious—just the way adults are bemused when children ask metaphysical questions which they really mean.

Joseph A. Tetlow, S.J., Ph.D. is president of the Jesuit School of Theology at Berkeley.

The Father: him I experience the way Huxley imagines we should experience nature's laws: which not only do not restrain and curtail, but which reward, being kept. The Father is, originates, is the substance of belief. He makes me wonder why he holds us off and does not show us his face, except as the other dimensions of the world's blocks. Why he is silent, I cannot say, except that his love is an uttered silence, and when he comes, anyone or anything else is a crashing noise. I am other than he only so that he can love again, and more. I would not otherwise be, and I would not have it be otherwise.

The perfect image of our Father is the prodigal's, running out to hug his child. He is the *patron* of an enormous *latifundio*, one of whose workmen has broken something in dereliction, one of whose infants has raised a ruckus in the kitchen. He receives the troubled worker and, untouched by the little trouble of something broken, sees only his man, and asks how he is, and his family. He embraces the child whose ruction in the kitchen was so great— but he, removed from the fluttering and clucking, receives the whole child, just as he is, just as he has done, and sits him on his lap. That is the Father, who embraces his world of humankind with all its brokenness, while setting afoot our healing.

The Son: an earthen vessel filled with radiance, the suffering servant who wants only to serve and is not allowed to. A little infant, a young man growing in wisdom, a very loving friend. And— not somehow, but as really as wheat becomes my flesh, when I eat it, so I his —still a lot of little infants and a lot of young growing in wisdom and a lot of very loving friends. Not myth, not metaphysics, not morality, but Jesus.

The Spirit: he is hardest, in some ways, although our own spirits are scored sometimes by his reading them to cry, "Abba, Father." Do the truth lovingly, and you will know him; do your lies, and he is as surely away as an absence in darkness. He comes unexpectedly and for no reason I can discern; then I am most sure of him. He comes because I can care about someone or someone about me; then I have to watch what the fruit is of this, and know him, though I am practiced by now and can tell the kind of fruit in its bud. He is surprise, like searing heat on a handle that looked merely dry; he is cool where you anticipated hasslement or fright.

So, God is the beginning now, though the wrestling is always about who is first. This is not a question of time, of chronology; he is clearly long before me and will be after me. It is a question of being, and my grasp is intermittent that he is, and I am nothing except in him. Sin is always at this point: I imagine that I have a will for myself apart from his and can make it stick, that I can reduce absurdity by the force of my own mind, and that I can come to be on my own. Merely trying this is its own punishment, now and hereafter.

About prayer, then: How? I pray most honestly when I know all of my own forces are unequal to anything I want or anything wanted of me. There being nothing else to do, I turn to him. He does not mind—I mean our turning to him when there is nothing else to do— because he is abject. Waiting is nothing to him, only the turning to him with half a heart or hypocritic one; he will not stand that. He does not hear what a hypocrite says; he reads beyond the hypocrite's lips, the hypocrite's heart, which is not calling out, but arguing. He does not argue, though he will wrestle as an honest thing. So I leave behind any thought that we can heal ourselves, even of silly things like adolescent lust or the yen for abstraction, or that the healing is our task. It is not —only sorrow, and joy, and praise.

Neither will he let me pray with the mind. It is the whole human he wants and the mind is good as memory, but worthless as the whole self. So to the extent that I can do what I am, I can pray. To the extent that I do what I am not, I go to prayer to ask him to heal what I am. In every case, *I go to prayer what I am*, or I need not go. The marvel is that he wants me as I am. I do not need to make myself other than I am before I pray; it is his work to make us other than we are, and prayer is when he likes to do it.

It is terrible to say these things, so familiarly, about him who is the Lord and master of everything that is and is surely not held in anyone's thoughts. O Lord, my guts turn to water when I hear myself talking as though I knew who you are and could tell you to come with me to bring you to another. But you do come; your Son has instructed us to call on you. Lord, I praise you that you have called on us only to love you, and not required of us that we understand.

Maybe here is another way of saying what prayer comes to: It is the self truly centered on God in the world. There is a secretness in it which makes no communication possible, yet makes communication the only natural consequence. As many experience it, there is no way to keep it quiet, this secretness with God, because it is the prism into which the world comes and from which it breaks into its truest colors for everyone to see.

The sources of prayer: Scripture, Ignatius' Exercises, Francis de Sales' *Introduction to the Devout Life*, Teresa's *Vida*. You learn after a while that God decides. He will be in a word or a tag of Scripture; he shows up in some great person's life, or in a liturgy, or in someone's depression or distress. He calls you where he wants you, and you learn to follow.

As for how it is done, it does not seem to me to matter how it is done, only whether the one who prays is wholly in it, finding God there, growing alert to the unauthentic ways he is given to of acting and not doing, learning consequences which he is to live out or else his prayer will evanesce into a vague wish to be himself. You never find yourself alone in prayer; you always find yourself in God. If you are afraid, he is courage; if you are crushed, he is wholeness; if you are a bundle of fragmenting distractions, he is lashing for the mind and heart. If you find something or someone else, you are not praying, you are doing something else—which may perhaps be profitable, though it is difficult to imagine that it could in any way be as profitable, finally, as finding God.

Then, there is the question of why? Why does prayer take you whole? Why does it weld you to the world and simultaneously make you indifferent to it?

You find that necessity—the kind Jesus meant when he said over and over again that he *must freely* lay down his life—you find that necessity is the Father. He is the ground, originating, and he is the law that says roses must smell sweet whether they want to or not, and that I must smell them only if I want to. Feel the imposition of time or of others' loves, labor under hot sun or pressures, be compelled by ungiving weaknesses—that is the Father. He made and makes the world, of things and of humankind; it is his life in them, and his liberty and kindness, his wanting and thirsting, his love. Bring any necessity to prayer, and you discover freedom, precisely because you discover that the necessity is the Father, and so is freedom. He orders all things sweetly from end to end; he is the ordering.

And when you turn to do this truth lovingly, you find yourself looking again and again into the face of Jesus. We are his body, members of one another, and he is truly, genuinely, among us. He has come into our human nature—not the way Paul did, or Einstein, though we may be glad of them, but uniquely, leading the Godhead into human flesh, our flesh, and into human knowing and loving, into our knowing and loving. We do what we do in Christ Jesus; we are making him come to be, now, in this moil, thinking thoughts and dreaming dreams and hoping hopes—in and for one another, even to the least among us. So we are doing the Word of the Father and keeping his light alive in human flesh,

and O God, it is beautiful to see him all around.

None of which we have power to do, or could even ask for it or even imagine it, but his Spirit is at work in us. Not as though he were a stonemason chipping away, but the way sound resonates in crystal and makes the crystal one with surroundings. If we see the face of Jesus in a friend's it is with the Spirit's vision, and if we rejoice to call the friend to life it is with the Spirit's joy. He reads our being and tells us who we are, and not one of us can explain how the sentences in Scripture come to burn away our wickedness, because he alone knows. He is the power who makes us one, and without him we would necessarily—perhaps with the exception of occasional giants —crawl about the world like mollusks and snails, never truly touching one another except to leave a scar. He, too, is therefore freedom.

All of this, in the end, would be gibberish, and we would have every reason to fear the scorn of the wise men and women of the world, except that once and for all God has proven to us that he understands our speech. With his own Word, he has validated our words—not only that we can talk with him, but that we can talk with one another, and his power—Power—will be in what we say. So may it please him now.●

"Be still and acknowledge that I am God"

ANNE E. PATRICK

Prayer doesn't concern me too much personally these days. That is, I no longer worry about it; in fact, sometime within the last decade (probably about five years ago) my efforts to gain proficiency in prayer sputtered out, and I more or less stopped trying to pray. Now I simply pray.

How do I know I'm praying? Well, I don't know for sure, but I'm *there*—in my room, in the church, or with a group in chapel or living room—and I'm not attending to anything else. In short, when I try to think of a word that describes what I'm doing and/or not doing during certain times, the best one I can come up with in English is "praying." When I wonder about this matter (when something nags inside me, "Are you really praying?") I've lately tended to give myself the kind of answer that sort of question deserves:

Anne E. Patrick, S.N.J.M. is presently a graduate student at the University of Chicago Divinity School.

"Anne, when the candle in your room is lighted, then surely you're praying. And probably at many other times also."

Some people are comfortable saying they "pray always," and only the intensity or kind varies. I don't find it helpful to think in such large terms. I sense a need to take time out occasionally, even daily, from everything but what is most real, and to regard this time specifically as "prayer." The Latin phrase, *desistite et agnoscite me Deum* sums it up.

I almost feel I must apologize for the last line, but I leave it as testimony to the mixed bag of religious language that is part of the equipment of those of us who never quite got over praying in Latin—nor expect to.

In any case, probably most of my prayer involves variations on this simple theme, "Be still and acknowledge that I am God." I find the "be still" part easier and easier as time goes on, certainly a vast improvement over the contortions I used to go through daily as a high school sodalist, and later as a novice and young teaching sister, to "place myself in the presence of God." These mental gymnastics served to exhaust the formal meditation time, but I've finally come to feel that this way of putting the opening into prayer ("let us place ourselves in the presence of God") connotes something about as useful or necessary as a mental effort to "place ourselves on the planet earth."

I should say more about why the "be still" aspect of prayer is central to me now. The reason has to do with my growing feminist awareness that the patriarchal language in which Christians have traditionally addressed and

thought about the divine reality is just not adequate. This realization has occasioned some of my greatest "problems" with prayer in recent years. While I want, for example, to articulate the religious disposition that underlies a song such as "Yahweh is the God of my salvation," the second line tends to stick in my throat: "I trust in *him* and have no fear." "Why must we always speak of God as 'he' or 'him'?" asks an automatic sexism detector in my consciousness. And, to add to the confusion, memory serves up some lines from a sermon by Rev. Peggy Way: "You are not my God, Jehovah! I will not *bow down* before a God who has men pray: I thank the Lord that thou hast not created me a woman. . . . I will not *worship* a God who only trusts his priesthood and his power and his prophecy to men." And yet I do want to worship the God of my salvation. It just seems easier, much of the time, to do this without words.

How has all this affected my day-to-day experience of prayer? Insofar as communal prayer and liturgy are concerned, I often find myself feeling like a stranger in what was once my homeland. There is a sense in which I would like to deactivate my sexism monitor for these times of prayer, but it's hard to turn off consciousness and still participate. It often ends up that my participation mainly involves reminding God of the alienation I feel on account of the way things have been for women in our tradition, and reminding myself that, paradoxically, the tradition itself affords grounds for hoping that things can someday be different.

Probably because liturgy and shared prayer (even the informal variety) have grown more problematic for me of late, I find that "private prayer" and "meditation" are assuming greater importance. Here it is sometimes possible to allow myself to be pushed back beyond thinking and talking to a region where the implications of "be still and acknowledge that I am God" can work themselves into my being—sometimes. Often I never get to the "implications," for all the time has been absorbed in the process of just growing "still."

In concrete terms, I sometimes find it helpful to read from the evening or night prayer in the *Prayer of Christians* (a volume also known as the "American Interim Brievary," which I've used since 1971) at the end of the day, but I ordinarily don't spend much time in prayer then. I find I do need to take time for prayer in the morning, however, and I usually rise early enough to allow forty minutes or an hour for prayer before the pressures and activities of the day demand my attention. What helps me to pray then? The fact that it's early, and quiet in the building, a cup or two of coffee, and, sometimes, a lighted candle.

I may begin by reading from the *Prayer of Christians*, or I may simply start by recalling what I have received in life, or by dwelling on something I believe. At times my worries about the coming day tend to encroach here, but I've discovered that by adding a "planning time"—perhaps ten minutes—at the conclusion of the "prayer time" it becomes fairly easy to defer practical decisions and considerations about what to do with the day ahead. However, I do not defer expressing my concerns and sense of need, and this sometimes comprises a good deal of the "prayer time."

There may come a point when I'll again be concerned with improving the "quality" of my prayer, but I'm currently downplaying this concern because, in the past, preoccupation with how well or how poorly I was doing proved much more of a block than a help to prayer. In general, I'd like to be better at living out a "theology of gifts," at living in the consciousness that the attitude commended by Jesus, "Do not be anxious. . . . Ask, and you shall receive," is in the end the only sane one. And thus I feel it makes sense to start by trusting that the kind of prayer one needs at any stage in life has in fact been given. ●

"The Spirit breathes where he wills"

M. BRENDAN McQUILLAN

Marie Brendan McQuillan, R.S.H.M., who lives at St. Mark's House of Prayer, is involved in giving retreats and in community development.

What Is Prayer?

What is prayer? There are probably as many answers to that question as there are pray-ers. To the question "What is time?" St. Augustine is said to have replied, "If you don't ask me, I know. If you ask me, I don't know." What is prayer?

I can only speak of my own experiences in prayer, of these things which have been helpful to me and to others with whom I have lived and prayed. I can only speak in terms of my own life, of what the Holy Spirit or those who have been his channels have shown me in prayer, of my relationship with our Father, with Jesus and with their Spirit.

Prayer and Decision

One of the most significant forms of personal prayer is the prayer of decision-making. Here, prayer and daily life converge. The style of life I have been living for more than six years, besides being a gift from God, is also the result of a decision made after a long and difficult period of prayer, a decision which opened the doorway to a new kind of life-style for me, a contemplative life.

In the winter of 1969 I spent a few months in retreat with a newly-formed contemplative community in South Bend, Indiana, where I learned much about prayer through praying, and through the simple life shared with the sisters. During those months I tasted the joy and satisfaction of a life of prayer and began to wonder how what I was experiencing could be carried over into the months ahead. I realized, too, that the pull to contemplation, to union with the Lord, to abiding in his love, had been with me for a long time, and I did not know what to do about it.

While I was struggling with those questions, a homily on Passion Sunday provided a great insight for me. The celebrant, reflecting on the Scripture of the day, said that he had always understood sharing in the passion of Christ as enduring some great trial or suffering, but that year he saw it not so much as what was done to Jesus as Jesus' own decision: "No one takes my life from me. I lay it down of my own free will" (Jn. 10:18). Participation in the passion of Jesus in our day, he said, is decision-making. In an age of openness such as ours, no one wants to make decisions. Religious communities hesitate to make decisions, chapters are reluctant to make decisions, individuals won't

make decisions. When you say "yes" to something you automatically say "no" to many other things. To imitate Jesus in his passion we must make whatever decisions the following of him demands. I realized that this was a word of grace and that I had to come to grips with the decision before me.

The ensuing struggle in prayer was intense and agonizing. I recall going out into the long field at the back of the house, at dawn, and as I walked up and down I wrestled with the Trinity, just begging the Father, Son and Holy Spirit to enlighten me, to direct me, to strengthen me—above all, to speak to me.

A word that I read in the Fathers of the Church was very helpful. I cannot recall the exact quotation or who said it. The sense of it, however, was that any decision of faith has ultimately to be made in darkness (even after we have gathered as much knowledge as possible) but when it is the right decision there is light when the leap in faith is made. As soon as I said "yes" to what the Holy Spirit seemed to be asking, to live a life of prayer, especially prayer of praise, the light foretold by the Church Father came and I experienced deep peace.

Solitude and Prayer

Arriving in Sag Harbor in September 1970, I lived alone for the first four months. Not that I had a call to be a hermit or that I believed that living alone was an ideal situation. However, the sister who wished to join me could not be freed from her college teaching duties until January. Through solitude, God provided the time for me to learn many things—about himself, about myself and others, about prayer and even about community.

First, I found it a rock-bottom experience to be without accustomed supports, without the safeguards that come from living with others. I was forced into a confrontation with myself, with existence, and with God in a very elemental way: I was thrown back ruthlessly on my own resources and from there hurtled, as it were, into the care, the protection and the mercy of God.

One of my earliest discoveries was the fact that for prayer I needed a schedule —a fairly rigid schedule, not only of time but of place. In former years we had had the communal support of prayer at scheduled times—meditation, examen of conscience, rosary, adoration, as well as morning and night prayer. Much of that had changed and prayer had become an individual responsibility. Now while living alone, praying the prayer of the Church at specific times, daybreak (morning praise), noon (midday prayer) and sunset (evening thanksgiving), provided a necessary framework for my day, even when the whole day was oriented more or less to prayer.

While I lived alone, the variety of persons, causes and concerns that came spontaneously into focus at prayer was wider than ever. A whole expansion of spiritual awareness accompanied an expanding sensory and psychological awareness. I often found myself praying for people I had not thought of in years and almost sensing their presence, or for something that had never entered the arena of my prayer-concern before. I had, in truth, a deeper sensitivity than ever before to "the joys and the hopes, the griefs and the anxieties of the men of this age, especially those who are poor or in any way afflicted" *(Gaudium et Spes).*

Scripture and Prayer

God speaks his Word not only in solitude but also when we are gathered together in his name to hear it. One of the characteristics of the charismatic renewal is a revived interest in and love for the Bible. My participation in the renewal, as well as my time in South Bend, helped to open up God's Word to me in a special way.

In the community in South Bend we spent much time praying the Scriptures. The evening dialogue of prayer focused on the liturgy for the following day. There as well as here in Sag Harbor this daily prayer is "daily bread," a powerful source of nourishment for me personally and for the community. "If you make my Word your home, you will indeed be my disciples; you will learn the truth, and the truth will make you free" (Jn. 8:31-32). Our communal resolution that follows the readings and is inspired by them is not usually concerned with "doing" something but rather with an attitude or a prayer for the group or for others that derives from the message of the liturgy.

God's Word is alive for us when it becomes one with our life. A teacher of retarded children and I were reading Scripture together one day. Judy—for that is the teacher's name—shared that she had read the Gospels frequently, had studied them in college, but was only beginning to see them in relation to her life. She gave an example from her teaching to show what she meant by connecting God's Word with her life. To teach the simplest word to any of her children is quite a task. Take the word CAT. After great effort and much time and repetition the child can say the word cat, spell C-A-T, read the word, and eventually write it. Then there comes a very special moment when that cat is identified with the little animal at home. Only when God's Word connects with our life do we really know his Word. I understood what Judy was saying and truly believed it, but I was to experience the truth of it during my retreat the following summer. I was meditating on Jesus in the desert (Lk. 4:1-13) and was praying about the three temptations. Luke recalls that Jesus "was tempted by the devil for forty days." I wanted to understand these temptations and Jesus' response to them so that I could imitate him when similarly attacked. I repeated the meditation a second and a third time, but it was only during the third hour that I allowed the Holy Spirit to show me what the lesson *he* wanted to teach me was. Not about the three temptations, but about what Jesus was doing in the desert. He was before his Father in prayer. It was so simple—so profound. And I remembered Judy's example. Suddenly and clearly the Word of God became one with my own life.

At times God's Word seems to speak more forcibly than at others. There are times when just one word, one phrase can have a tremendous impact. Easter Sunday 1971 was such an occasion. The preceding Holy Week had been a rich one: rich in prayer because of a retreat held at Cormaria (the retreat house close to St. Mark's where I live); rich in companionship because many of my sisters were making the retreat and they had asked me to share prayer with them, and also because a former student had come from Denver, Colorado, to spend the week in prayer with me; rich in liturgy because of the meaningful Holy Week celebrations. Then came Easter Sunday afternoon.

The liturgy was over; the retreat had ended and everyone had gone home. I was alone again and as I walked along the beach about three in the afternoon (I recall that the beach was deserted except for two small children who persuaded me to pick stones and shells with them for a while) it seemed that being alone was not the best way to celebrate the greatest day of the year.

When I returned to St. Mark's, I opened the Jerusalem Bible. Ordinarily, before opening the Bible, I ask the Holy Spirit to direct me to a word of counsel or comfort. This time I opened it almost mechanically, without much prayer or expectation. The lines before me were: "He has told me, 'You are my son, today I have become your father'" (Ps. 2:7). It is impossible to put in words what I felt then, what joy filled my heart, what illumination flooded my entire being. Instantaneously my loneliness gave way to the deepest relationship I have ever experienced. My emptiness was so filled with God's love that I had to express it. I began writing down the lines, designing them on paper, then on the stones and shells I had brought in from the beach. "You are my son"—daugher?—no, son. When the Father sees me, he sees Jesus, therefore, "son." "You are my son, today—Easter Sunday 1971, the day of the exaltation of the risen Jesus. I have become your Father." Since that time these words have been powerfully present to me and the reality that God is my Father is predominant in my life. It is a frequent subject of prayer and a never-ending source of strength, of consolation and of grateful joy.

What Is Prayer?

The Holy Spirit, master of prayer, uses many ways to teach us how to pray: through our own experience, through solitude, through the Word of God, through others. "The Spirit breathes where he wills." "And because we are sons, God has sent the Spirit of his Son into our hearts, crying 'Abba! Father!'" All prayer is resumed in that mystery of relationship between Father, Son and Holy Spirit. When we believe and yield to their love in us, we have begun to answer the question: What is prayer? ●

ERNEST L. UNTERKOEFLER

"Always pray and do not lose heart"

To open one's prayer life to public view can bring many risks of misinterpretation. Looking at the overall development of my prayer relationships, I find strength, weakness, progress and retrogression. Over the decades, each has contributed to the other.

Most Reverend Ernest L. Unterkoefler, S.T.L., J.C.D. is Bishop of Charleston.

At the outset, prayer experiences reflect a profile of self and an understanding of God's unique presence and movements in my life. For a long while, it seemed that prayer as a means of conversation and communication satisfied my approach to God. Can my prayer be dialogic? Basically, my awareness of God's presence in my life experience turns toward a deeper understanding of God and self.

Approaches to fruitful prayer have importance for me. Before I enter a period of prayer, I try to work out mentally why I am praying. What is my purpose and will it be a faithful expression of my love for God? Am I worthy of God's love? Easiest of all is the approach to liturgical prayer, the celebration of the Eucharist and sacrament. Yet the preparation for public prayer is very demanding. Refining attitudes enters into the careful understanding of the event in which Christ meets all.

What I mean is that fruitful prayer requires that I be free from concerns that move my inner self inward rather than outward in the expression of my ministry of liturgical celebration among the people. With the acceptance of the principles and experience of liturgical reform and renewal, I know that I am more sensitive to the atmosphere of the community in prayer. Deeply I feel that my inner renewal of spirit depends on a faithful expression of my sincere communion in Christ. When my conviction about myself can be revealed, the people who participate may respond in faith and love with a concern about interior renewal of prayerful enthusiasm. They respond in faith to the Father; I must help them. In this community celebration, I am glad, sad, enthusiastic, meditative, vocal. I speak, think, sing and express the simplicity and compassion of Christ. The community can assess my prayerfulness, my mood, my concerns and, over a period of time, how responsive I am to the Holy Spirit. My liturgical ministry is central to my growth in communion with Christ and my understanding that the time, energy, thought and preparation I give to liturgical prayer is a means of my priestly relationship with God and the people. I become richer in my personal experience of the rhythm of the suffering, death and resurrection of the Lord in my life.

The paschal mystery influences my thoughts and deeds. My hope for many years urges me to see to it that this great mystery generates a transcendent element in the process of my decision-making for the local Church. What I proclaim in public worship relates to my pastoral care of our people in South Carolina.

Next to the celebration of the liturgy, the recitation of the Liturgy of the Hours provides me with a period of reading the psalms, hymns, passages of Sacred Scripture, prayers of intercession and honoring the mysteries of our faith and the lives of saintly persons. There is a continuity of themes that gives me some vision of the problems of the day, the decisions to be made, the tensions to resolve. Morning Prayer, Midday Prayer and Evening Prayer mark the phases of each day. No day is the same as I approach God the Father for care, wisdom, grace and understanding. My faith becomes enriched and those relationships I have in faith—e.g., with Christ, the Church, the people of God, our Holy Father, my fellow bishops, priests and deacons —are understood more deeply.

As I begin the Liturgy of the Hours, I read, "Thus in the heart of Christ the praise of God finds expression in human words of adoration, propitiation and intercession; the head of renewed humanity and mediator of God prays to the Father in the name of and for the good of all mankind" (No. 3, General Instruction, Liturgy of the Hours).

The renewed form of the Liturgy of the Hours affords me an ordered means of readings of Sacred Scripture, the writings of the Fathers and saints. In fulfilling my mission as preacher and teacher, I rely on these daily readings to nourish my spirit.

Most of the time I am alone with my book of prayer, but there are occasions when I am with others. Infrequent are the opportunities I have to pray in community in monasteries and convents. These experiences in prayer with men and women religious are special times of the Father's goodness.

Christ teaches me what it means to be alone in prayer; the desert prayer supports my solitude. Away from the busy pattern of life, free from a time schedule, the Lord speaks. Those great levels of prayer of contemplation become open to the Lord. I am given a share in a transfiguration of spirit which makes the mystery of the transfiguration so real.

The experience of contemplation flows into action when I am transformed into a man of prayer, mercy and patience. The real difficulty lies in the short memory which does not impede a proneness to fall. In those moments I say, "God, be merciful to me, a sinner." The ups and downs of prayer life challenge me to follow Christ, to unite suffering and rejoicing with him.

Places of Prayer

Jesus gave us some insight into the value of the environment in which we pray. He prayed in the desert, in the hills, in the synagogue. As a bishop, places of prayer are varied and sometimes unusual—airports, bus stations, trains, churches in the city and in the rural areas. At home and many times away from home, when it is difficult to meditate because of noise, reading the prayers becomes more suitable. The number of interruptions can bring one to a decision to turn to other things. I find that prayer is more congenial when the degree of concentration rises to awareness of the presence of God. Faith is alerted to a more stable and persevering communion with God. The personhood of Jesus Christ captures memory, imagination, mind, heart and will in his presence in the Blessed Sacrament. The peace brought about in visits with the Lord in the Eucharist is indicative of the harmony and order of society that could come about when all are united in Christ.

Persons and Prayer

Praying with priests offers a communal sharing of prayers that brings a dimension of unity. As priests, our prayers develop characteristics different from lay persons. Our prayers become different, not necessarily better or worse. I have a tendency to pray for persons, the sick, the poor, the isolated, etc. In this I must constantly remind myself that I am a member with them in the mystical body of Christ; I am urged to go to them. Does my prayer become too action-oriented? Then I say there is a connection between prayer and witness. I am not authentic if I separate them continuously or show that witness may be independent of prayer, or that prayer never reaches out in witness. It is so easy to become an extremist when the beautiful Christian balance of prayer and witness is altered so that they are made exclusive of one another. Some days I can be more alive to witness than to prayer in the strict sense. Other times the universal attractiveness of prayer gives direction to action. I am encouraged in this my evaluation by the words of Pope Paul VI: "Sometimes, in the anxiety of our modern mentality to get things done, we are inclined to consider that one, prayer, is an obstacle to the other, action: as if they were competing for time, now scarce, and forces made more precious by the acceleration of our polyvalent activity. In fact, they are and must be complementary, according to ancient Benedictine wisdom, *ora et labora,* pray and work; and above all, according to the evangelical mandate: 'Always pray and do not lose heart' " (Lk. 18:1).

Difficulty in Prayer

Even though I have deep convictions about God, Christ as a person, the Church, my baptism, confirmation and sacred orders, at no time would I dare to minimize the difficulties in stabilizing at a certain level of prayer. I have experienced retreats where I knew the growth level of my prayer life. But then new difficulties arise.

Pastoral duties and prayer are intimately related. When I interview men for the seminary, dialogue with our vocation direction, and read mail from our seminarians, I find my prayers involving their lives, their aspirations and hopes.

God works with us in prayer; he brings about our prayer when we pray. Normally, our openness to God's love and care will allow his communication in our circumstances of living for us. God does speak to us as we are—persons who are free, growing, sinful and capable of redemption. Prayer gives us such an insight into the real self that God's truth is proclaimed in our lives. This is when we hedge, give excuses

and project a variant image of self. We have difficulty in accepting ourselves at the ground level of our being in union with Christ.

Special Occasions

Days just before ordinations to the diaconate and priesthood have a special character in my prayerful life. I pray for myself as the one appointed and trusted for the laying on of hands. I review in prayer the day of my ordination, read again the prayers, hymns, readings, the Eucharistic celebration. The ordination, basically the same in doctrine, will have a unique understanding in the life of each deacon or priest. My prayerful union with the Lord for a forthcoming ordination will reflect itself in the ceremony. I must be open to the great action of God in this mystery of sharing the priesthood of Jesus Christ.

Retreat time is a personal and intimate period of the whole spectrum of types of prayer—the liturgy, the Hours, communal shared prayer, charismatic prayer, private reflection, meditation, contemplation. Prayer at retreat time has an overwhelming influence on me; this occurs when giving retreats and when participating as a member and leader of a body of priests. More than usual, the Holy Spirit strengthens us in prayer, guides and enlightens.

The confirmation season finds me preparing in prayer to communicate faithfully to the candidates, their families and friends. It is a time when I submit my ministry and life to the Holy Spirit. For my personal growth in prayer, this season of the Holy Spirit brings me many supernatural helps. How much more I am aware of the grace of God. I pray that God will care for the candidates and their families. Confirmation celebrations are a time of grace for me; I do sense a closer bond with the Spirit. My hope is that the Holy Spirit is pleased with me.

Anguish, joy and hope can best describe my experience in prayer with our brothers and sisters of communions which are Christian. My ecumenical work has persevered because of prayer.

Anguish rises when there is a clear, visible sign of our separation; joy and hope are special features of prayers which inspire the search for unity. Common prayer with our Christian friends enriches the determination to be open to the Spirit as we are moved toward Christian unity.

Prayer with our Jewish neighbors allows me to sense the great visions of Abraham, Isaac and Jacob. Their concrete communication with Yahweh paves the way for understanding how present is God who is Love.

I feel strongly that people should celebrate sacred jubilees, e.g., anniversaries of marriage, ordination, profession in religious life. These are occasions when people are invited and attracted to pray. As the presiding celebrant on these occasions, I find a style of prayer which makes love of one another a visible reality in my life. Love is a sacred sacrament of life. I rejoice with my brothers and sisters. I praise the Lord more enthusiastically.

Though I have no claim to being "charismatic," I do recognize charisms of the Spirit for a rich prayer life. Suffering is part of that life. I have never been authentic in prayer without being mindful of the *cross*. I accept it as inevitable because it is part of my discipleship with Christ.

I could go on to express my prayerful expressions in preparing for sacramental celebrations, for funerals, public and civic ceremonies.

In summary, though not successful, I strive to reach a level of prayer in all undertakings. How many times I fail is known to others and many times to me. I am sorry for the times I fail to pray properly or when I so easily forget the climate of prayer to which I am basically committed.●

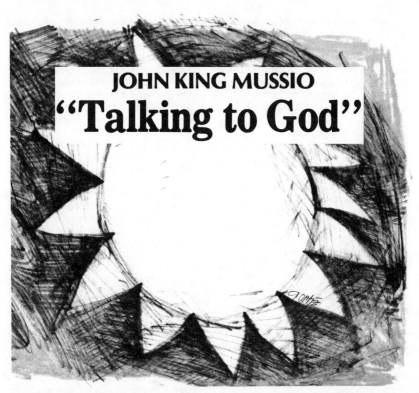

JOHN KING MUSSIO
"Talking to God"

I grew up in a family where prayers were as much a part of our living as were home-made fudge on Friday nights and cottage ham with cabbage on washdays. We didn't engage in much common prayer at home because it was not often that we were all at home at one time. But we did pray together in church on Sundays and at Benediction on Fridays, we visited the churches on Holy Thursday and there prayed for indulgences, we made the Three Hours on Good Friday, we attended the "wakes" of our departed

friends and prayed together the rosary for their peace of soul. At home we did our praying privately and we were encouraged in our own private devotions by the knowledge that what we did in private was also being done by the others. We were not a family of puritanical living but one that enjoyed what we had and thanked God for blessing us with our happiness and contentment.

I was the impulsive one. There were times when I had bursts of gratitude, moments when I was so flooded with the beauty and the excitement of the joy of living that I had to say what was

Most Reverend John King Mussio, J.C.D. is Bishop of Steubenville.

in my heart right then and there. And I did just that in my own words peppered with the enthrallment of my spirit. It was a prayer conversational in style and intimate in expression. But I got off my chest what I had in mind and felt. And when, with time, I realized that the Lord was becoming closer to me, that his person was dearer to me, and that my religious observances were becoming more a part of me, I dared to say to myself that these "one to one" talks were indeed to the liking of my Lord.

As I passed the days and years I found these intimate talks with God were easing the tensions of my growing up. I just told the Lord how I felt, what bothered me, and what I thought he could do to help. I assured myself that God would not be offended by my openness in prayer as long as I was trying to be pleasing to him and to retain his love for me. I didn't think he would object to my talking to him from my heart, in all sincerity and in basic truthfulness. Yet I kept these prayers, these talks, to myself because they were too intimate to expose to the attention of others. Anyway, they belonged to God alone.

I began this talking to God when I was about ten years old. I recall the day when I went to my parents' bedroom to kiss them goodnight. When I opened the bedroom door I saw my father on his knees praying his night prayers. Somehow or other this sight warmed me with a great inner personal peace. Today as I look back I think what affected me was the realization that with my father on such good terms with God the family was secure and I need never fear being an outcast from a broken home. I remember going back to my room and saying to God with all the familiarity of a friend of long standing: "Thank you, God, for my father. It was good of you to give him to me when there were so many others you might have blessed with his goodness." This came from my heart and I didn't need structured words to say what I felt. I recall another time when prayer sprang to my lips. My mother would come into my bedroom at night to kiss me goodnight. As she leaned over my pillow her hair would fall down over my face leaving me and her together in a sort of sweet smelling tent. What else could I say to God but words of thanks for happiness and joy. "How happy you make me, God, and how glad I am that I can know your love for me in the kiss and embrace of my dear mother." These were the two occasions I remember that began for me a lifetime of talks with God, conversations, if you will, or, perhaps you might prefer to say in a modern word, dialogue. But whatever you name it, I was saying to God exactly what I felt and wanted him to know. This much I can say for "talking to God"—it drew me closer to the Father and the Father to me. The more I thanked him for all the good things of my life, the more I realized how much he must love me. And when you get to this point, then God becomes to you something more than a name. He is the One who walks with you all day long. And as you walk you talk with all the sincerity of friends who love one another.

Yet during these days of my talking to God I was always a little fearful that perhaps I might be offending God by not addressing him in the archaic forms of formal prayer. I know I had always been taught to speak respectfully to my elders and to show them the deference their years deserved. Was I being respectful to God by blurting out my joys, my excitements, my desires, my wants and my thanks? Was God offended that I did not use the "thous" and "thees" so often used when addressing him? Was I boring the Almighty by monopolizing his ear with my own prattle about the day's happenings as well as filling him with my own problems and needs? Was I offering competition to the Church when I took God aside and centered his attention on my needs instead of being concerned about the common need? These things bothered me for a while, but little by little I became aware that God was becoming more and more a real friend of mine. Surely this couldn't be bad. Then I recalled the incident of Christ's praying in the garden of Gethsemane. "And they came to a country place called Gethsemane and he said to his disciples, 'Sit down here, while I pray.' And he took with him Peter and James and John, and he began to feel dread and to be exceedingly troubled. And he said to them, 'My soul is sad even unto death. Wait here and watch.' And going forward a little he fell on the ground, and began to pray that, if it were possible, the hour might pass from him; and he said: 'Abba, Father, all things are possible to thee. Remove this cup from me, but yet not what I will but what thou willest.' "

Now this is the kind of talking to God that I have been talking about. Christ had something to say privately to his Father that others might not understand or might even be scandalized were they to hear of his fears and low spirit. So Jesus left his disciples behind and went alone to talk to his Father. And he didn't say the prayer he had given to his disciples as a perfect prayer but spoke to the Father in words which revealed the worrying fears that now beset him. This speaking intimately to the Father settled his spirit. It was then that he arose and went out to meet his

betrayer. If ever there was in the life of Christ a time when he needed the assurance that his Father understood him in his human fears and was pleased with his acceptance of the mission given to him, this was the time. It was a moment of shared confidence between God and man. Christ spoke to God his Father in words that rose from his troubled spirit. And after this came peace.

Now this incident in the life of Christ settled my own problem. Talking to God could not be wrong if it brought God closer to me, made him someone I loved, someone I would never think of offending simply because he was too good to me to be hurt.

When I arrived at the age to shave I found talking to God so much a part of my prayer life that to throw it aside would have been to lose a God-relationship which is today my comfort and my strength. I talked to God as I walked to school. I would tell him what were my problems and how I intended to work them out. I didn't ask him to do what I knew was my own job but I did ask him to help me. I made it a point to tell him that what I planned to do was for his pleasure; otherwise I didn't want it to succeed. Sometimes I wondered if people watching me walk to school would think that I was a bit "touched" when they could see my lips trying to catch up with my thoughts. Even to this day as a bishop I walk to my office with a lot to tell the Lord. Mostly this consists in "thank you's" for the graces of the day, and for his help in furthering projects designed to give our people what they need for their proper religious service. I still tell the Lord that what I ask of him is what I seek for the spiritual good of his children. And I still tell him that if I am asking out of pride, ambition, or personal profit, forget it. And sometimes he does.

We need personal prayer and sometimes we need it desperately. For one thing we can almost lose ourselves in the magnitude of the creation that makes us seem like insignificant dots on the map of human destiny. We can without vigilance fall into the error of those who say that God is too remote from us to know or care about us as individuals. Or that we have no place in the pattern of creation save to live and die according to the blueprint of human existence. If we fall into a bad mood we can at times feel ourselves lost in the glob of humanity which surrounds us and we can wonder how anyone, even God, could be interested in one insignificant creature in an ever recurring generation of countless millions of people. We need to be reassured that God is our Father and that his interest in us is that of one who made us to find happiness and peace in a union of love with him. His love for us is on a "one for one" basis. Personal prayer, since it is a dialogue between two persons, is our assurance that we are not lost in a sea of humanity but the love-object of a concerned God. Personal prayer, then, becomes the revelation of intimacies between loved ones. I thank God all the time in formal prayer for the understanding that I developed from these talks I have with him. And then he in turn talks to me and I hear his voice in the sense of the contentment and security which comes to my spirit when I realize just who I am, where I am going, and who awaits me there.

Begin the practice of talking to God by thanking him for sun-bursting mornings and star-glittering nights. You will be amazed how many blessings come to you each day from the hand of God. Your friends warm you with their consideration and concern. Your neighbors show kindness and strive to save you the troubles that come with duty. You grow old without worry, you suffer sickness without undue fear. You find your plans go awry and yet you build again. You call nothing failure as long as God gives you the strength to try again. All things are in your power to accomplish if they are for God's glory and with his help. Keep thanking God for all his favors during the day. Then you will see him as the true friend he is. Who can resist the spirit of those who do good to us? And so it is that you begin to experience a love for God that produces in you a love-return. When you know that God loves you beyond measure, you inaugurate in yourself a life of love, a giving of self that reaches the level of sainthood. It all doesn't happen in a flash, but it is the beginning of that sanctity to which we are all called. Being grateful for God's gifts to you puts you in touch with God. You hold his hand, you feel his presence, you read his heart, you trust him enough to open your own heart and tell him the secrets of your soul. Talking to God is walking with God. And walking with God is going where he leads.

We all need someone, a treasured friend, to be always at our side. Why not ask God to be that someone? Talk to him; pray in a manner in keeping with your nature, your needs, your temperament and your age. We pray formally when as a member of society we ask God for what we need to secure our society in justice, brotherhood and the observance of human rights. Prayer in common is also desirable that we might know the needs of our fellow men and women and join with others in giving what we can for their needs. There are times when we must gather together as the people of God and recognize him as our leader and as our Lord. And there are times when we want God to know that we are alive and active in his service, that we have our own personal needs, and that we are helpless without the grace and favor of his attention. Then it is that we knock on his door, seek his compassion, ask of him the love of a friend.

When you feel this need, when your lips are trembling with the urgency of your words, when your heart is bursting with the fervor of your devotion, then you talk to God in your own words, with the passion of your need, and in the openness of your trust. No one need teach grief how to cry or joyfulness to laugh. When something comes up within you that cries to be said, say it. You can be sure that his ear is open to your prayer and his heart is warm with love for you.

To me this is personal prayer in its simplest exercise of communion with God. And it has this bonus: little by little you become, without doubt, a person of prayer. Now unless I am mistaken, this is another definition for a saint of God. I think Daniel of old had this practice of talking to God because he recounts this incident in his own writing: "I was still speaking, still at prayer . . . when Gabriel flew suddenly down to me" (Dan. 9:20). Now what about that! ●

"The love that the Father has lavished on us"

RICHARD BOULET

As I reflect on my personal experience and understanding of prayer, I find myself confronted with a myriad of thoughts and feelings, all deeply rooted, closely interwoven, and not easily sorted out. The thought occurs to describe prayer as love has been described, as a "many splendored thing," for prayer means many things, signifies many things, is many things. When try-

ing to answer what prayer means to me, I feel somewhat like the father in *Fiddler on the Roof* trying to answer, after all those years, why and how he loved his wife.

Seeking to express the meaning of prayer in relationship to love seems appropriate, as prayer for me is intimately associated with love, is the language of love. In some ways describing one's prayer experience is as difficult as trying to discuss the multi-facetedness of love itself. It is like trying to describe a

Dr. Richard A. Boulet is director of the Department of Religious Studies at the University of Dayton.

friendship or a friend of long standing, something that has been with me for a long time. It is hard to pinpoint accurately all the aspects of the friendship. On the one hand it is utterly simple, and yet, on the other, it is quite complex. Like so many relationships of long standing, it has had its ups and downs, undergone growth, needed cultivation, and been a source of strength. At the same time it has been something which I have run the danger of taking for granted and not appreciating as fully as I should.

Prayer is in great measure an acknowledgment of dependency, of indebtedness. It is the recognition of the many gifts received from God in Jesus Christ and his Spirit, gifts of life and health, of faith, love, family, friendship, etc. The dependency is continual and, so, too, should be prayer (Lk. 18:1). For me prayer is the expression of gratitude, of thanksgiving. It is the response of love rooted in the belief in the goodness of God and the gratuity of his personal love. At the same time it is an expression of need for continuing help to acknowledge this dependency and to respond to the Spirit dwelling in me. The pitfalls are the ever present dangers of not taking the time to reflect upon one's indebtedness or to acknowledge it and of attributing good fortune to one's own self-sufficiency.

Prayer is also the language of friendship. It is communication with Jesus Christ who has called us friends (Jn. 15:5). It is a conversation with the Trinitarian God dwelling within us (Jn. 14:23ff.). It is a simple sharing of one's self, thoughts, hopes, and needs with a trust in the promise that we will be heard (Mt. 7:7). Prayer is really something marked by the attitudes of faith, hope, and love. I am convinced that prayer is our response as persons to the divine friendship extended to us as Christians. A key danger in this instance is that of taking this friendship for granted, failing either to acknowledge it or to cultivate it. We have to set time apart to be with one's friends, to sustain and to deepen one's love and understanding.

Prayer is "presence." Just as our friends go with us wherever we are, so, too, in a more profound way, God's presence is ever with us. When I say prayer is "presence," I mean it is our awareness of God's presence to us and our sense of being with him. It is communing with God deep within us; it is also communing with him as he is in others. For me a very special place to be aware of God, to be with him, to be "present," is found in nature itself. To use the ocean as an example, the creator himself can be perceived everywhere: in the vastness of the ocean, the restlessness of the tides, the power of the surf, the majesty of the sky, the beauty of the sunset over the water, the wisdom of it all. Prayer for me is being with God and with him in persons and nature. The task is to provide the time for the awareness and the enjoyment of this presence. To be able to enjoy it we have to be willing to be silent in order to commune. At times our own insecurity leads us to fill in that silence, fearful perhaps of the demands, or subtle requests, that the friendship with God will make upon us. Not taking the time to listen, so great a pitfall in human communication, is particularly a problem in the life of prayer. Time simply has to be made for silent listening that we may hear the promptings of the Spirit.

In addition to some of the problems already noted, I think one of the major difficulties is conceiving of prayer as a task to be completed. Prayer is simply not something "to be done." Though it is important to set aside time for prayer and reflect upon the truths of faith, the simple passage of an allotted amount of time or the reflection on a certain number of points is not prayer. If prayer is conceived as a task fulfilled in the accomplishment of certain mathematical requirements, we can fail to see that the essence of prayer rests in, and flows from, personal attitudes which dispose us to respond to "the love that the Father has lavished on us" (1 Jn. 3:1).

Finally, I find it is important to keep in mind the injunction of our Lord to pray to our Father in secret, lest I "imitate the hypocrites" (Mt. 6:5). Coming apart to reflect, converse, and commune, away from distractions, is essential. When troubled as to the adequacy of my prayer, I find it comforting to recall that "the Spirit comes to help us in our weakness. For when we cannot choose words in order to pray properly, the Spirit himself expresses our plea in a way that could never be put into words" (Rom. 8:26).●

ADULT EDUCATION PROGRAM

BY SARA AND RICHARD REICHERT

GENERAL INTRODUCTION

The purpose of this educational supplement is to provide a practical plan for adult religious education. This plan will be based on selected articles from each issue of NEW CATHOLIC WORLD and will provide adult education programs for eight weeks.

Each session will be built upon key articles and will explode outward from these experiences, information, and group techniques.

1ST WEEK PROGRAM

A. INTRODUCTION

—AIM:

To relate the need for personal prayer/contemplation with the call to action/service.

—Participants should have read Rosemary Ruether's article.

—Materials: Copies of a current newspaper, one copy for each group of six to eight participants; Bibles; paper and pencils.

B. EDUCATIONAL PLAN

1. Introduction (10 minutes)

a. Leader asks participants to review main ideas of article, and summarizes, stressing the need for integration of private prayer and public/communal existence and responsibility.

b. Divide participants into groups.

2. What's the Problem? (30 minutes)

a. Groups review together the local newspaper and identify an article they agree expresses a social problem that they all feel a responsibility to try to solve.

b. Once identified, each gives a spontaneous/first impression solution what they as individuals or as a group could or should do to resolve it. These are recorded, at least by a generalized expression, phrase or sentence.

3. With Prayer (30 minutes)

Persons are asked to spend the next thirty minutes praying over the problem. Bibles are offered as an aid but not required.

Note: this may seem like a long time but it is useful for the purpose of demonstrating that they can actually "pray" for that length of time if given a real need for assistance or guidance.

4. Integration (20 minutes)

a. In small groups and then in large groups participants share any new insights they received by the period of prayer. Typical questions for starting the discussion include: If you review your group's first reaction, what would you now reinforce? What would you change?

b. Leader ends by making the point that we are called to be active pray-ers and prayerful activists.

2ND WEEK PROGRAM

A. INTRODUCTION

—AIM:

To discover how Christ prayed and when he prayed in order to grow in awareness of our own opportunities for prayer.

—Participants should have read Francis J. Buckley's article.

—Materials: Paper, pencils and Bibles, newsprint and felt pens.

B. EDUCATIONAL PLAN

1. Introduction (10 minutes)

a. Leader explains the overall purpose of the session (cf. Aim, above) and asks for volunteers to give general impressions of how and when Jesus prayed, based on their recollections of Scripture.

b. Participants are divided into groups of six to eight.

2. Bible Search/Personal Search (60 minutes)

a. Individually, participants scan the Gospels looking for instances recording Jesus at prayer or speaking of prayer. In each instance they jot down pertinent details: when, where, why, how, as recorded in Scripture.

b. Next, individually participants now jot down instances where they prayed during the last week: when, where, why, how.

c. Next, participants share these results in two columns on newsprint under two headings: "Jesus Prays" and "We Pray."

d. Each group shares results with total group and then enter general discussion to determine to what degree the group's personal prayer parallels that of Jesus. Areas for improvement are identified.

3. Personal Diary (15 minutes)

a. Individually participants make a calendar of anticipated situations for the next week citing situations under three headings for each day: Morning—Noon—Night. Then they asterisk those where they think they might have the best opportunities for prayer.

b. As an optional activity they are invited to share these anticipated diaries with others to look for comparisons.

4. Conclusion (5 minutes)

Leader asks participants to keep these diaries for the next week—not to be shared—marking those instances where they actually prayed.

Close with a recitation of the Our Father, but with the group adding "Teach us to pray" after each of the seven petitions—e.g., Our Father, who art in heaven—teach us to pray. Hallowed be thy name—teach us to pray, etc.

3RD WEEK PROGRAM

A. INTRODUCTION

—AIM:

To review and re-evaluate various forms of personal prayer and also evaluate one's personal prayer habits.

—Participants should have read articles by Whealon and Dorothy Donnelly.

—Materials: Paper, pencils, prayer can (see below), matches.

B. EDUCATIONAL PLAN

1. Introduction (20 minutes)

Leader or invited speaker gives a short review of the various kinds of prayer mentioned in the articles, plus the values/obstacles to each:
—Meditation (generalized method)
—Office
—Mass (viewed from personal vs. communal aspect)
—Morning and Evening Prayers/Prayer formulas
—Rosary
—Meditative Reading

2. Pick Your Own (30 minutes)

a. Divide participants into basic interest groups/life-styles: e.g., housewives, business people, elderly, etc.

b. Each group discusses the pros and cons of each prayer style to discern if anyone feels a particular kind is adaptable to his/her situation more than another.

3. Sharing (30 minutes)

Groups share results, using the following kinds of questions as a stimulus:

(a) Can we say a particular prayer form is more suitable to one group than to another?
(b) Are prayer forms a personal decision or are they imposed by culture/society?
(c) Does this restrict one's possibilities for personal prayer by implying we have to pray in one of these ways?

4. Conclusion (10 minutes)

a. Each person makes a resolve to improve his/her prayer life and writes this resolve on a piece of paper.

b. Papers are placed in an already ignited prayer can (coffee can decorated suitably) while all sing together the Prayer of St. Francis.

4TH WEEK PROGRAM

A. INTRODUCTION

—AIM:

To review opportunities and means for praying in a typical family setting.

—Participants should have read Doris Donnelly's article.

—Materials: Papers, pencils, newsprint, felt pens.

B. EDUCATIONAL PLAN

1. Introduction (10 minutes)

Leader asks participants to recall main points of article or offers a brief review.

Divide participants into groups of six to eight.

2. Home Life/Prayer Life (30 minutes)

a. Each group is asked to identify times and occasions where family prayer could most naturally be introduced. These are summarized in two columns: "Times" and "Occasions."

b. Groups share with total group. A gestalt of results is placed on newsprint.

3. How (40 minutes)

Each group, now using this gestalt, attempts to suggest ways/formats/methods in which a family could actually pray at these various times and occasions.

4. Sharing (10 minutes)

Each group now shares the three best ideas they feel they have identified as opportunities or means for family prayer.

5TH WEEK PROGRAM

A. INTRODUCTION

—AIM:

To help people become more open in sharing their own prayer experiences with others in a non-threatening manner.

—Participants should have read the entire magazine.

—Materials: Copies of current issue of *New Catholic World*, paper and pencils.

B. EDUCATIONAL PLAN

1. Introduction (5 minutes)

Each person is given a copy/brings a copy of the magazine. All present are asked to review it and then identify the one article that best expresses their own feelings and/or practice regarding personal prayer.

2. Reflection (20 minutes)

a. All present are asked to review the current issue, on the assumption they have read it. If they have not, time is still sufficient to become acquainted with some articles.

b. They are asked to jot down and be prepared to give a

short response to this question: Which article comes closest to expressing your personal experience of and attitude toward personal prayer?

3. Testimonials (60 minutes—less in a smaller group)

a. Each person in turn is asked to share his/her conclusions as to the best article in terms of expressing personal experience or attitude and why that choice was made.

b. If time permits or in a smaller group a general discussion can follow by asking this question: Is there a best way to pray when it comes to personal prayer?

4. Conclusion (5 minutes)

Leader simply asks for spontaneous answers to these two questions: Did you gain insights from hearing how others discussed their own attitudes toward prayer? Should this kind of sharing be done more often within the Church?

6TH WEEK PROGRAM

A. INTRODUCTION

—AIM:

To demonstrate that even private prayer has a certain common dimension that illustrates a common humanity and a common human need to pray.

—Participants should have read the entire magazine.

—Materials: Copies of current issue of *New Catholic World*, paper and pencils, newsprint and felt pens.

B. EDUCATIONAL PLAN

1. Introduction (10 minutes)

a. Leader divides participants into groups of six to eight.

b. Each group is assigned five articles from the current issue at random—e.g., Group One: 2, 4, 6, 8, 10; Group Two: 1, 3, 5, 7, 9; Group Three: 12, 14, 16, 18, 20, etc.

2. Common Cause (50 minutes)

a. Each group reviews its assigned articles and attempts to list what all five have in common in these two areas: "Manner of Prayer" and "Assumptions about Humanity."

b. These items should be reduced to three in each column!

3. We Are How We Pray (25 minutes)

a. All groups share conclusions and attempt to come to a consensus as to why human beings pray the way they do, and why they pray at all.

b. Total group develops a symbol that expresses the human being praying.

4. Conclusion (5 minutes)

Ask each participant to pray, *but* only after assuming a bodily position that for him/her expresses what he/she captured in the group's symbol. (Play in the background a recording of "The Impossible Dream.")

7TH WEEK PROGRAM

A. INTRODUCTION

—AIM:

To develop a "prayer manual" for the parish or group that the participants represent.

—Participants should have read the entire magazine.

—Materials: Paper and pencils, forms (see below), copies of current issue of *New Catholic World.*

B. EDUCATIONAL PLAN

1. Introduction (10 minutes)

Leader explains purpose of session after presenting this form:

Definition of Personal Prayer
Times
Occasions
Places
Aids
Forms/Styles/Formats
Obstacles

Each group is to develop a prayer manual by filling in the outline in specific detail.

Groups are formed—six to eight in each.

2. Work Session (50 minutes)

Each group completes its outline, developing a manual of personal prayer.

3. Editing (20 minutes)

a. Groups share results.

b. Groups edit their own "manuals" based on input of other groups.

---

4. Publishing (10 minutes)

a. Groups are asked to share ideas on what to do with their "manuals" (e.g., each could be published in parish bulletin in coming weeks, etc.).

b. Follow-up sessions planned as needed.

8TH WEEK PROGRAM

A. INTRODUCTION

—AIM:

To integrate private prayer with communal prayer.

—Participants should have read Unterkoefler's article.

—Materials: Whatever is necessary for celebration of a liturgy, plus Bibles.

B. EDUCATIONAL PLAN

1. Introduction (30 minutes)

Leader asks group to plan a liturgy together to include these aspects of planning:

a. theme related to prayer and/or the prayer
b. readings
c. songs
d. special actions, gestures
e. setting/decorations

2. Reflection (20 minutes)

After planning and preparations are completed, each individual is asked to go aside—with Bible if desired—to reflect upon what is about to be celebrated.

3. Celebration (30 minutes)

4. Conclusion (10 minutes)

Group is asked to review what has happened this particular evening by asking this question: Did the time for private preparation enhance or hinder the communal celebration?